W9-ASU-973

ALSO BY JOHN BERGER

A Painter of Our Time
Permanent Red
The Foot of Clive
Corker's Freedom
The Success and Failure of Picasso
A Fortunate Man (with Jean Mohr)
Art and Revolution
The Look of Things
G.
Ways of Seeing
A Seventh Man (with Jean Mohr)
About Looking
Pig Earth
Another Way of Telling

FILM SCRIPTS

Salamander
The Middle of the World
Jonah Who Will Be 25 in the Year 2000

PLAYS

A Question of Geography (with Nella Bielski)

And our faces,
my heart,
brief as photos

And our faces,
my heart,
brief as photos

John Berger

PANTHEON BOOKS   NEW YORK

Copyright © 1984 by John Berger
All rights reserved under International
and Pan-American Copyright Conventions.
Published in the United States by Pantheon Books,
a division of Random House, Inc., New York,
and simultaneously in Canada by Random House
of Canada Limited, Toronto.
Portions of this book previously appeared, in somewhat
different form, in *The Village Voice*.
Library of Congress Cataloging in Publication Data
Berger, John.
And our faces, my heart, brief as photos.
I. Title.
PR6052.E564A82   1984   828'.91407   83-24941
ISBN 0-394-53738-6
ISBN 0-394-72427-5 (pbk.)
Book design by Camilla Filancia
Manufactured in the United States of America
First Edition

I would like to express my solidarity with the Transnational Institute, Amsterdam, and the Institute of Policy Studies, Washington, D.C., and to thank them for their support and encouragement during all the years when this book was being conceived and written. I would also like to thank *New Society*, London, and *The Village Voice*, New York, for publishing a number of articles in which I worked out some of the ideas envisaged for this book. Finally I would like to thank Anthony Barnett for his critical help.

Part One is about Time.

Part Two is about Space.

1/Once

When I open my wallet
to show my papers
pay money
or check the time of a train
I look at your face.

The flower's pollen
is older than the mountains
Aravis is young
as mountains go.

The flower's ovules
will be seeding still
when Aravis then aged
is no more than a hill.

The flower in the heart's
wallet, the force
of what lives us
outliving the mountain.

And our faces, my heart, brief as photos.

ONCE UPON A TIME

The first was a hare. At two thousand meters on a mountain frontier. Where are you going? asked the French cus-

toms officer. To Italy, I said. Why didn't you stop? he asked. I thought you beckoned me on, I replied. And at that moment everything was forgotten because a hare ran across the road, ten yards away from us. It was a lean hare with tufts on the tips of its ears of brown smoke. And although it was running slowly, it ran for its life. Sometimes that can happen.

A few moments later the hare ran back across the road, this time pursued by half a dozen men, who nevertheless were running much slower than it, and who had the air of having just jumped up from a meal. The hare ran upwards towards the crags and the first patch of snow. The customs man was shouting instructions about how to catch the hare—and I drove on, over the frontier.

The next animal was a kitten. An entirely white kitten. It belonged to a kitchen with an uneven floor, an open chimney, a wooden table that was somewhat broken, and rough white-washed walls. Against the walls the kitten was almost invisible except for its dark eyes. When it turned its head away, it disappeared into the wall. When it jumped about over the floor or onto the table, it was like a creature that had escaped from the walls. The way that it appeared and disappeared gave it the mysterious intimacy of a household god. I have always thought that household gods were animals. Sometimes visible and sometimes invisible, but always present. As I sat at the table, the cat jumped onto my legs. It had sharp white teeth as white as its fur. And a pink tongue. Like all kittens it played continually: with its own tail, on the backs of the chairs, with scraps on the floor. When it wanted to rest, it looked for something soft to lie on. And watching it, fascinated, throughout a week, I observed that, whenever it could, it chose something white—a towel, a white pull-over, some washing. Then, with eyes shut and mouth closed, curled up, it became invisible, surrounded by the white walls.

A village in the hills, not far from Pistoia. The village cemetery was rectangular with high walls round it and wrought-iron gates. At night most of the gravestones were lit up, each with its individual candlelight. But the candles were electric, and they were switched on with the street lamps. They burnt all night and there were many more of them than street lamps in the village. Just past the cemetery, the road turned sharply and, at the bend, a dust road led off to a farm. On this dust road I saw one of the grey ducks.

On several occasions I had seen the whole family. They often installed themselves on the grass bank under the bushes opposite the cemetery. The first time I saw the cemetery lights at dusk, I noticed the ducks waddling around in the night-green grass. A duck, a drake and about six ducklings.

This time it was only the drake, stationary, in the middle of the road, pawing the dust, with his head down. It took a minute or so before I realized that he was on the back of the duck, who was entirely invisible. Once or twice she spread her wings out and they appeared under his feet, before she settled down again, into the dust. His thrusts became faster. Finally, having reached his climax, the drake fell off the duck and she became visible. He fell off her sideways onto the road. He fell as if he had been shot, lying on his side. A small bird-shaped grey bag, inert in the dust, as if full of lead. She looked around, got to her feet, beat her wings, stretched her neck and wandered off, confident that the ducklings would now find her.

One night, walking in the countryside near Prijedor in

Bosnia, I found a solitary glow-worm, with its amber-green light, under some grasses. I picked it up and carried it on my finger where it glowed like an electric opal on a ring. When I approached the house the other lights competed too strongly, and it put its own out.

In the bedroom I placed it on some leaves on top of the chest of drawers. When I put the light out, the glow-worm glowed again. At the back of the dressing table was a mirror which faced the window. If I lay on my side I saw a star reflected in the mirror and the glow-worm beneath on the chest of drawers. The only difference between them was that the light of the glow-worm was slightly greener, more glacial, further away.

ONCE IN A STORY

We are both storytellers. Lying on our backs, we look up at the night sky. This is where stories began, under the aegis of that multitude of stars which at night filch certitudes and sometimes return them as faith. Those who first invented and then named the constellations were storytellers. Tracing an imaginary line between a cluster of stars gave them an image and an identity. The stars threaded on that line were like events threaded on a narrative. Imagining the constellations did not of course change the stars, nor did it change the black emptiness that surrounds them. What it changed was the way people read the night sky.

The problem of time is like the darkness of the sky. Every event is inscribed in its own time. Events may cluster and their times overlap, but the time in common between events does not extend as law beyond the clustering.

A famine is a tragic cluster of events. To which the Great Plough is indifferent, existing as it does in another time.

The life span of a hare on one hand and a tortoise on the other are prescribed in their cells. The likely duration of a life is a dimension of its organic structure. There is no way of comparing the time of the hare with that of the tortoise except by using an abstraction which has nothing to do with either. Man introduced this abstraction and organized a race to discover which of the two would reach the finishing post first.

Man is unique insofar as he constitutes two events. The event of his biological organism—and, in this, he is like the tortoise and hare—and the event of his consciousness. Thus in man two times coexist, corresponding with these two events. The time during which he is conceived, grows, matures, ages, dies. And the time of his consciousness.

The first time understands itself. Which is why animals have no philosophical problems. The second time has been understood in different ways in different periods. It is indeed the first task of any culture to propose an understanding of the time of consciousness, of the relations of past to future realized as such.

The explanation offered by contemporary European culture—which, during the last two centuries, has increasingly marginalized other explanations—is that which constructs a uniform, abstract, unilinear law of time applying to all events, and according to which all "times" can be compared and regulated. This law maintains that the Great Plough and the famine belong to the same calculus, a calculus which is indifferent to both. It also maintains that human consciousness is an event, set in time, like any other. Thus, an explanation whose task is to "explain" the time of consciousness, treats that consciousness as if it were as passive as a geological stratum. If modern man has often become a victim of his own positivism, the process starts here with the denial or abolition of the time created by the event of consciousness.

In reality we are always between two times: that of the body and that of consciousness. Hence the distinction made in all other cultures between body and soul. The soul is first, and above all, the locus of another time.

What astounds cannot be
the remnant of what
has been.
Tomorrow still blind
advances slowly.
Sight and light
race towards each other,
and from their embrace
is born the day,
eyes open
tall as a foal.

Murmuring river
clasps the mist
for a moment more.
The peaks are signing on
the sky.
Stop and hear
the milking machines
designed to suck like calves.
In the first heat
the forested hills calculate
their steepness.
The lorry driver is taking the road
to the pass which leads
surprisingly
with its own familiarity
to another homeland.
Soon the grass will be
warmer
than the cows' horns.
The astounding comes
towards us
outrider of death and birth.

When in 1872 Marx wrote, "A spectre is haunting
Europe—the spectre of Communism. All the Powers of old
Europe have entered into a holy alliance to exorcise this
spectre: Pope and Czar, Metternich and Guizot, French Rad-
icals and German police spies," he was making a double announcement. The rich feared revolution, as they still fear it

today. The second announcement was of a different order. It was a reminder that every modern society is aware of its own ephemerality.

History since the French Revolution has changed its role. Once it was the guardian of the past: now it has become the midwife of the future. It no longer speaks of the changeless but, rather, of the laws of change which spare nothing. Everywhere history is seen as progress, sometimes sociopolitical progress, and continually technological progress. History rightly offers hope to the desperate and the exploited struggling for justice. (In the Third World, as the century approaches its end, this hope is increasingly joining forces with religious faith.) In the world of the relatively rich, history's unique and insatiable demand has become that of obsolescence.

Thus people live a new temporal dimension. Social life which once offered an example of relative permanence is now the guarantor of impermanence. Given the actual condition of the world, this offers a promise. But equally, it means that people find themselves more alone than they used to be, before the enigma of the two times of their lives. No social value any longer underwrites the time of consciousness. Or, to be more exact, no accepted social value can do so. In certain circumstances—I think of Che Guevara—revolutionary consciousness performs this role in a new way.

Often when I shut my eyes, faces appear before me. What is remarkable about them is their definition. Each face has the sharpness of an engraving.

I related this experience once to a friend. He said he was

sure it must be connected with the fact that during my life-
time—I was in my thirties when it first happened to me—I
had looked at and concentrated upon so many thousands of
paintings. This seems very likely. But it sidesteps the real
issue, because the principal function of painting, until recently, was to depict, to make as if continually present, what
soon was to be absent.

None of the faces is ever familiar to me. Usually they are
fairly still, but they are not static images; they are alive. They
are like the face of a person thinking. They are clearly not
aware of my watching them. Yet I am able to make them
look at me. "Make them" is perhaps too strong a term: it
requires no great effort on my part. Instead of simply watching a group of them, I have to concentrate my attention on a
particular one and then she or he, as frequently happens in
daily life, looks up and returns my gaze. Their optical distance away from me is normally about three or four meters,
but when one returns my gaze, her or his expression is such,
its intensity is such, that our faces might be only a few centimeters apart.

The expression, although modified by the face's character
and age, is always similar. Its intensity is not a question of
emotion, or of pleasure or pain. The face looks straight at me
and without words, by the expression of the eyes alone, it
affirms the reality of its existence. As if my gaze had called
out a name, and the face, by returning it, was answering,
"Present!"

I am always aware that if I open my eyes, the faces will
immediately disappear, become absent. What is less clear to
me is what happens when I shut my eyes. Is it I who cross
the barrier that normally excludes them, or is it they who
cross it? They belong to the past. The certainty with which I
know this has nothing to do with their clothes or the "style"
of their faces. They belong to the past because they are the

dead, and I know this by the way they look at me. They look at me with something approaching recognition.

I was in that state between waking and sleeping. From there you can wander towards either of the two. You can go away in a dream or you can open your eyes, be aware of your body, the room, the crows cawing in the snow outside the window. What distinguishes this state from that of full wakefulness is that there is no distance between word and meaning. It is the place of original naming. And from there I saw myself before birth, more than nine months before birth. The life-to-come in the womb was further away perhaps than death is now.

To be conceived was a call to come forward, to assume a form. Yet this prior existence, although formless, was neither vague nor neuter. (I say neuter rather than neutral for it had a sexual charge, that of an undifferentiated sexuality.) I was placeless and so innocent. I was unparticular and so invulnerable. But I was also happy. The only image of this happiness, the only contraband I could smuggle back across the frontier of full wakefulness, was not an image of myself—for that surely did not exist on the other side of the frontier— but an image of something akin to myself: the flat surface of a rock, a stone over which a skin of water flowed continuously.

We are both storytellers. Lying on our backs, we look up at the night sky.

Where is Tony Goodwin now? His death proclaims that he can never again be present anywhere: that he has ceased to exist. Physically this is true. In the orchard they were burning leaves two weeks ago. I walk through the ashes when I go down to the village. Ashes are ashes. Tony's life now belongs, historically, to the past. Physically his body, simplified by burning to the element of carbon, re-enters the physical process of the world. Carbon is the prerequisite for any form of life, the source of the organic. I tell myself these things not in order to concoct a specious alchemy of immortality, but in order to remind myself that it is my view of time which is being remorselessly cross-examined by death. There is no point in using death to simplify ourselves. Tony is no longer within the nexus of time as lived by those who, until recently, were his contemporaries. He is on the circumference of that nexus (the circumference not of a circle but of a sphere) as are diamonds and amoebas. Yet he is also within that nexus as are all the dead. They are there as all-that-the-living-are-not. The dead are the imagination of the living. And for the dead, unlike the living, the circumference of the sphere is neither frontier nor barrier.

The pulse of the dead
as interminably
constant as the silence
which pockets the thrush.

The eyes of the dead
    inscribed on our palms
as we walk on this earth
which pockets the thrush.

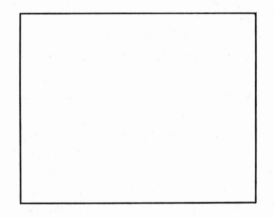

The photograph which lies on the table in front of me has
become incriminating. Better not to print it—even thousands
of miles away from Turkey. It shows six men standing in a
line, in a wooden-panelled room somewhere on the outskirts
of Ankara. The photo was taken after a political committee
meeting, two years ago. Five of the men are workers. The
eldest is in his fifties, the youngest in his late twenties.

Each one is as unmistakably himself as he would be in the
eyes of his own mother. One is bald, one has curly hair, two
are thin and wiry, one is broad-shouldered and well-covered.
All are wearing skimpy, cheap trousers and jackets. These
clothes bear the same relation to the suits of the bourgeois as
the capital's shantytowns, where the five live, bear to the

villas with French furniture where the bosses and merchants live.

Yet, with their clothes taken off, in a public bath, a police or army officer would have little difficulty in identifying them as workers. Even if the five half-closed their eyes so as to mask their expressions, so as to pretend to a commendable indifference, their social class would still be evident. Even if with the magical aid of certain *djinn* they assumed, with consummate art, the typical facial expression of a speculator's mistress—an expression of sugared charm, sugared indifference and greed—the way they hold their heads would still betray them.

It is as if a court, at the moments of their conception, had sentenced them all to have their heads severed from their necks at the age of fifteen. When the time came, they resisted, as all workers resist, and their heads remained on their shoulders. But the tension and obstinacy of that resistance has remained, and still remains, visible—there between the nape of the neck and the shoulder blades. Most workers in the world carry the same physical stigma: a sign of how the labor power of their bodies has been wrenched away from their heads, where their thoughts and imaginings continue, but deprived now of the possession of their own days and working energy.

For the five in the wood-panelled room, resistance is more than a reflex, more than the muscles' primitive refusal of what the body knows to be an injustice—because what its effort is continually creating is immediately and irredeemably taken out of its hands. Their resistance has mounted, and entered their thoughts, their hopes, their explanations of the world. The five heads, whose eyes pierce me, have declared their bodies, not only resistant, but militant.

Since the coup d'état of September 1980, DISK—the left confederation of trade unions, to which the five belonged—

has been declared illegal, as indeed have all political parties.

At least 50,000 people have been arrested. The prosecution has demanded hundreds of death penalties—particularly against militant trade unionists. The manhunts are as systematic as the torture used in the hope of extracting further names and connections. This is why the photograph has become incriminating.

Thousands have disappeared without news. To date at least eighty have died under torture. It is probable that one of the five I'm looking at is being tortured today. His body, so unmistakable in his mother's eyes, is being made to suffer the unthinkable.

How much this photograph says about politics! About how politics, at their origin, are irrepressible. These five men, with their loves, their children, their songs and their Anatolian memory, are the dupes of nobody. They were often badly led, often carelessly organized, often the first victims of the charismatic self-indulgence of their leaders, but none of this has surprised them. Of this present world which they know so well, they did not expect better.

They know that there has never been a winter in Anatolia without snow, a summer without animals dying from drought, a workers' movement without repression. Utopias exist only in carpets. But they know too that what they have been subjected to in their lives is intolerable. And the naming of the intolerable is itself the hope.

When something is termed intolerable, actions must follow. These actions are subject to all the vicissitudes of life. But the pure hope resides first and mysteriously in the capacity to name the intolerable as such: and this capacity comes from afar—from the past and from the future. This is why politics and courage are inevitable. The time of the torturers is agonizingly but exclusively the present.

If I screen out the heads in the photo of the five men in

the wood-panelled room, it is no longer incriminating. One sees only the skimpy clothes, the hands, the open collars. But headless like this, their bodies are trapped in the present of their torturers. . . . . . . Ahmed, Salib, Mehmet, Deniz, Kerime . . . it will end.

An angel in white stone, whose wing tips merge, in the winter light, with the high hawk-colored cliff behind the village—this stone angel holds the wrist of a soldier, whose legs have already given way, and who is slumping into death. The angel does not save him, but appears somehow to lighten the soldier's fall. Yet the hand which holds the wrist takes no weight, and is no firmer than a nurse's hand taking a pulse. If his fall appears to be lightened, it is only because both figures have been carved out of the same piece of stone.

On the plinth below are inscribed the forty-five names of the men who fell in the war between 1914 and 1918. Then, on another face of the plinth, twenty-one further names were added after the Second World War. Seven of these last were deported and died in German concentration camps, others were machine-gunned within earshot of the war memorial. All were in the Maquis. Some, before they died, were tortured in the Pax hotel at Annemasse, the local headquarters of the Gestapo. Did the guardian angel with the nurse's hand appear in that renowned hotel or in the camps of Mauthausen, Dachau, and Auschwitz?

Amongst these men, many, at different moments, had a vision of a morning in the future when they would walk again, indelibly scarred but carefree, through the village of their country which had been freed. The stone angel, if she represents anything, represents that morning.

July 16th, 1981, 11 A.M. I did not see the cities of the future or their new technology. Nor did I see the collapse of these cities. What I saw had nothing to do with prophecy.

I saw only the village street, which is so familiar to me that I could walk down it blindfolded if I had a stick. A blind man died a few years back. Blind from birth, he could walk down to the village from the hamlet where he lived four kilometers away. The bees he kept gave more honey than any others in the village. And he axed his own wood on a chopping block, without ever cutting his hand.

At 11 A.M. it was sunny with a blue sky. The few white clouds were moving fast above the mountains. A north wind.

I saw the village street at that moment, as seen from the future. What I was seeing had become the distant past. This transformation was calm, so calm that it resembled a stillness.

The men and women in front of the Mairie, where the Tricolor was flying, were now an image in the minds of their descendants. They had acquired the mystery and the stability of the past. They had attained a kind of a complete incompleteness. They were waiting to be completed by the knowledge and actions of their descendants. And, at the same time, they were complete for they had completed themselves: they could do no more.

I saw the future as the blind man saw his way down to the village.

Sometimes, I'd like to write a book
A book all about time
About how it doesn't exist,
How the past and the future
Are one continuous present.
I think that all people—those living,
     those who have lived
And those who are still to live—are alive now.
I should like to take that subject to pieces,
Like a soldier dismantling his rifle.

wrote Yevgeny Vinokurov.

ONCE IN A POEM

Poems, even when narrative, do not resemble stories. All stories are about battles, of one kind or another, which end in victory and defeat. Everything moves towards the end, when the outcome will be known.

Poems, regardless of any outcome, cross the battlefields, tending the wounded, listening to the wild monologues of the triumphant or the fearful. They bring a kind of peace. Not by anaesthesia or easy reassurance, but by recognition and the promise that what has been experienced cannot disappear as if it had never been. Yet the promise is not of a monument. (Who, still on a battlefield, wants monuments?) The promise is that language has acknowledged, has given shelter, to the experience which demanded, which cried out.

Poems are nearer to prayers than to stories, but in poetry there is no one behind the language being prayed to. It is the language itself which has to hear and acknowledge. For the religious poet, the Word is the first attribute of God. In all poetry words are a presence before they are a means of communication.

Yet poetry uses the same words, and more or less the same syntax as, say, the Annual General Report of a multinational corporation. (Corporations that prepare for their profit some of the most terrible battlefields of the modern world.) How then can poetry so transform language that, instead of simply communicating information, it listens and promises and fulfills the role of a god?

That a poem may use the same words as a Company Report means no more than the fact that a lighthouse and a prison cell may be built with stones from the same quarry, joined by the same mortar. Everything depends upon the relation between the words. And the sum total of all these possible relations depends upon how the writer relates to language, not as vocabulary, not as syntax, not even as structure, but as a principle and a presence.

The poet places language beyond the reach of time: or, more accurately, the poet approaches language as if it were a place, an assembly point, where time has no finality, where time itself is encompassed and contained.

If poetry sometimes speaks of its own immortality, the claim is more far-reaching than that of the genius of a particular poet in a particular cultural history. Immortality here should be distinguished from posthumous fame. Poetry can speak of immortality because it abandons itself to language, in the belief that language embraces all experience, past, present, and future.

To speak of the promise of poetry would be misleading, for a promise projects into the future, and it is precisely the coexistence of future, present, and past that poetry proposes.

A promise that applies to the present and past as well as to the future can better be called an assurance.

ONCE IN AMSTERDAM

It is strange how art historians sometimes pay so much attention, when trying to date certain paintings, to "style," inventories, bills, auction lists, and so little to the painted evidence concerning the model's age. It is as if they do not trust the painter on this point. For example, when they try to date and arrange in chronological order Rembrandt's paintings of Hendrickje Stoffels. No painter was a greater expert about the process of aging, and no painter has left us a more intimate record of the great love of his life. Whatever the documentary conjectures may allow, the paintings make it clear that the love between Hendrickje and the painter lasted for about twenty years, until her death, six years before his.

She was ten or twelve years younger than he. When she died she was, on the evidence of the paintings, at the very least forty-five, and when he first painted her she could certainly not have been older than twenty-seven. Their daughter, Cornelia, was baptized in 1654. This means that Hendrickje gave birth to their child when she was in her mid-thirties.

The *Woman in Bed* (from Edinburgh) was painted, by my reckoning, a little before or a little after the birth of Cornelia. The historians suggest that it may be a fragment taken from a larger work representing the wedding night of Sarah and Tobias. A biblical subject for Rembrandt was always contemporary. If it is a fragment, it is certain that

Rembrandt finished it, and bequeathed it finally to the spectator, as his most intimate painting of the woman he loved.

There are other paintings of Hendrickje. Before the *Bathsheba* in the Louvre, or the *Woman Bathing* in the National Gallery (London), I am wordless. Not because their genius inhibits me, but because the experience from which they derive and which they express—desire experiencing itself as something as old as the known world, tenderness experiencing itself as the end of the world, the eyes' endless rediscovery, as if for the first time, of their love of a familiar body—all this comes before and goes beyond words. No other paintings lead so deftly and powerfully to silence. Yet, in both, Hendrickje is absorbed in her own actions. In the painter's vision of her there is the greatest intimacy, but there is no mutual intimacy between them. They are paintings which speak of his love, not of hers.

In the painting of the *Woman in Bed* there is a complicity between the woman and the painter. This complicity includes both reticence and abandon, day and night. The curtain of the bed, which Hendrickje lifts up with her hand, marks the threshold between daytime and nighttime.

In two years, by daylight, Van Rijn will be declared bankrupt. Ten years before, by daylight, Hendrickje came to work in Van Rijn's house as a nurse for his baby son. In the light of Dutch seventeenth-century accountability and Calvinism, the housekeeper and the painter have distinct and separate responsibilities. Hence their reticence.

At night, they leave their century.

A necklace hangs loose across her breasts,
And between them lingers—
        yet is it a lingering

and not an incessant arrival?—
the perfume of forever.
A perfume as old as sleep,
as familiar to the living as to the dead.

Leaning forward from her pillows, she lifts up the curtain with the back of her hand, for its palm, its face, is already welcoming, already making a gesture which is preparatory to the act of touching his head.

She has not yet slept. Her gaze follows him as he approaches. In her face the two of them are reunited. Impossible now to separate the two images: his image of her in bed, as he remembers her: her image of him as she sees him approaching their bed. It is nighttime.

ONCE IN A PAINTING

Paintings are static. The uniqueness of the experience of looking at a painting repeatedly—over a period of days or years—is that, in the midst of flux, the image remains changeless. Of course the significance of the image may change, as a result of either historical or personal events, but what is depicted is unchanging: the same milk flowing from the same jug, the waves on the sea with exactly the same formations unbroken, the smile and the face which have not altered.

One might be tempted to say that paintings preserve a moment. Yet on reflection this is obviously untrue. For the moment of a painting, unlike a moment photographed, never existed as such. And so a painting cannot be said to preserve it.

In early Renaissance art, in paintings from non-European cultures, in certain modern works, the image implies a passage of time. Looking at it, the spectator sees Before, During, and After. The Chinese sage takes a walk from one tree to another, the carriage runs over the child, the nude descends the staircase. Yet the ensuing images are still static whilst referring to the dynamic world beyond their edges, and this poses the problem of what is the meaning of that strange contrast between static and dynamic. Strange because it is both so flagrant and so taken for granted.

When is a painting finished? Not when it finally corresponds to something already existing—like the second shoe of a pair—but when the foreseen ideal moment of its being looked at is filled, as the painter feels or calculates it ought to be. The long or short process of painting a picture is the process of constructing such a moment. Of course, the painting's moment-of-being-looked-at cannot be entirely forseen and thus completely filled by the painting. Nevertheless every painting is, by its very nature, addressed to such a moment.

Whether the painter is a simple practitioner or a master makes no difference to this address of the painting. The difference is in what the painting delivers: in how closely the moment of its being looked at, as foreseen by the painter, corresponds to the interests of the actual moments of its being looked at by other people, when the circumstances surrounding its production (patronage, fashion, ideology) have changed.

Some painters when working have a habit of studying their painting, when it has reached a certain stage, in a mirror. What they then see is the image reversed. If questioned about why this helps, they say that it allows them to see the painting anew, with a fresher eye. What they glimpse in the mirror is perhaps a little like the look of their painting at that future moment to which it is being addressed.

All finished paintings, whether a year or five hundred years old, are now prophecies, received from the past, about what the spectator is seeing in front of the canvas at the present moment. Sometimes the prophecy is quickly exhausted—the painting loses its address; sometimes it remains persistently true.

Yet why is the still imagery of painting so compelling? What prevents painting being patently inadequate—just because it is static?

To say that paintings prophesy the experience of their being looked at does not really answer the question. Such prophecies assume a continuing interest in the static image. Why, at least until recently, was such an assumption justified? The conventional answer is that, because painting is static, it has the power to establish a visually "palpable" harmony. Only something which is still can be so simultaneously composed, and therefore so complete.

A musical composition, since it uses time, is obliged to have a beginning and an end. A painting only has a beginning and an end insofar as it is a physical object: within its imagery there is neither beginning nor end. This is what makes possible pictorial composition, harmony, form.

The terms of the explanation seem to me to be both too restrictive and too aesthetic. There has to be a virtue in that flagrant contrast: the contrast between the unchanging painted form and the dynamic living model.

Could it not be that the stillness of the painted image speaks of timelessness? The fact that paintings are prophecies of themselves being looked at has nothing to do with the perspective of modern avant-gardism, whereby the future is always vindicating the misunderstood prophet. What the past, the present, and the future share is a substratum, a ground of timelessness.

The language of pictorial art, because it is static, is the language of such timelessness. Yet what it speaks about—unlike geometry—is the sensuous, the particular, and the ephemeral.

A sailor receives a letter
from a thousand versts away.
His wife has written
that in their house
beyond the cliffs
she is happy.

And this *is* of her letter
during evenings with girls
in untranslatable ports,
through the sea of the months
persuades the cursing sailor
that his never-ending voyage
will end.

ONCE IN A LIFETIME

It started with a small hillock, a little above and to the north of a field where I was raking hay. On this hillock were three neglected pear trees, two in full leaf and one with its grey wood, leafless and dead. Behind them, the blue sky with large white clouds.

This small corner of the landscape—which I had never particularly noticed before—caught my eye and pleased me. Pleased me like a particular face one may see passing in the street, unknown, even unremarkable, but for some reason pleasing because of what it suggests of a life being lived.

Soon afterwards I had the impression of being watched. For an instant I believed there was somebody standing on the hillock, or that a boy had climbed into one of the pear trees. The dead one was flanked by the two living ones. Yet there was nobody there.

When a man surprises an animal, or vice versa, the track of their gaze momentarily excludes everything else. It was like that, except that between animal and man there is usually an equality of presence, and there I was aware of an inequality. I was less present than the corner of the landscape which was watching me.

The three pear trees looked different. The articulation of every branch had become apparent, I could see how each leaf moved. (All afternoon the north and south winds were contesting one another in gentle, brief breezes, scarcely longer than a breath.) The ground under the pear trees had changed.

Until I met you, I would have been unable to name the transformation that was taking place. Today, at my late age, I name it—the fusion of love.

Everything was shifting. The three pear trees, their hillock, the other side of the valley, the harvested fields, the forests. The mountains were higher, every tree and field nearer. Everything visible approached me. Rather, everything approached the place where I had been, for I was no longer in that place. I was everywhere, as much in the forest across the valley as in the dead pear tree, as much on the face of the mountain as in the field where I was raking hay.

ONCE THROUGH A LENS

Suppose a character, in one of the stories you and I write, tried to conceive of his origin, and tried to foresee beyond what he knows of his destiny at any given point of the story. His enquiries, his speculations, would lead him to hypotheses (infinity, chance, indeterminacy, free will, curved space and time . . .) very similar to those at which thinkers arrive when speculating about the universe.

This is why the traffic between storytelling and metaphysics is continuous.

The notion that life, as lived, is a story being told is a recurring one. Rationalism rejected this notion by proposing that the laws of nature were ineluctably mechanical. Most recent scientific research tends to suggest that the natural working of the processes of the universe resemble those of a brain rather than a machine. To think of such a "brain" as a narrator—although many scientists would protest that the thought was too anthropomorphic—has again become feasible. The metaphysics of storytelling has ceased to be a merely literary concern.

What separates us from the characters about whom we write is not knowledge, either objective or subjective, but their experience of time in the story we are telling. This separation allows us, the storytellers, the power of knowing the whole. Yet, equally, this separation renders us powerless: we cannot control our characters, after the narration has begun. We are obliged to follow them, and this following is through and across the time, which they are living and which we oversee.

The time, and therefore the story, belongs to them. Yet the meaning of the story, what makes it worthy of being told, is what we can see and what inspires us because we are beyond its time.

Those who read or listen to our stories see everything as through a lens. This lens is the secret of narration, and it is ground anew in every story, ground between the temporal and the timeless.

If we storytellers are Death's Secretaries, we are so because, in our brief mortal lives, we are grinders of these lenses.

ONCE IN CHILDHOOD

Thumb in mouth as sleep comes. The taste of one's own body enveloping one, like sleep. No harm comes from one's own body.

Rage. Filling with cries a cavern of fear or anger. The cries, like red leaves, floating in the air, independent of oneself, and yet settling on one, covering one's face, provoking further cries.

Being comforted after crying. The bellows in one's stomach stop blowing. A still sweetness, like liquid honey, accumulates in the chest. Only the roof of the mouth is still sore. The inexplicable cause has inexplicably vanished.

The inability to remember is itself perhaps a memory. One lived with the experience of namelessness: there were certain elemental forces—heat, cold, pain, sweetness—which were recognizable. As also a few persons. But there were no verbs and no nouns. Even the first pronoun was a growing conviction rather than a fact, and because of this lack, memories (as distinct from a certain functioning of memory) did not exist.

Once one lived in a seamless experience of wordlessness. Wordlessness means that everything is continuous. The later dream of an ideal language, a language which says all simultaneously, perhaps begins with the memory of this state without memories.

My heart born naked
was swaddled in lullabies.
Later alone it wore
poems for clothes.
Like a shirt
I carried on my back
the poetry I had read.

So I lived for half a century
until wordlessly we met.

From my shirt on the back of the chair
I learn tonight
how many years
of learning by heart
I waited for you.

ONCE IN AUXONNE

The post office at Auxonne is small and the postmistress has blue eyes. I have been there only twice.

The first time was to send you a parcel; as the postmistress weighed it on the scale, I imagined your hands opening it.

"Four kilos, three hundred grams."

In a parcel, wrapped by hand, there is a message weighing nothing: the receiver's fingers may unknot the string which the sender's tied.

In the post office I saw in my mind's eye your fingers untying the knot I tied at Auxonne.

Ten days later I again stopped in the town, and went to the post office, this time to post you a letter. I remembered the day when I sent off the parcel and I felt a twinge of loss. Yet what had I lost? The parcel had arrived safely. You had made soup with the beetroots. And the bottle of distilled water from the flowers of orange trees you had placed on its shelf, above your dresses in the cupboard. All that had been lost was the little future of the parcel.

What we mourn for the dead is the loss of their hopes. The man-with-the-parcel was as if dead; he could hope no more. The man-with-the-letter had taken his place.

ONCE IN THE PAST

One's death is already one's own. It belongs to nobody else: not even to a killer. This means that it is already part of one's life. Not just in the sense that it may be anticipated and prepared for, but in the sense that its content is already, at least partly, determined. This, in the past, was the key of clairvoyance. Later new claims of freedom discredited all determinism. The notion of absolute freedom accompanied the birth of linear historical time. Such freedom was the sole consolation. Yet only when time is unilinear does the foresee-ing of a future event or the pre-existence of a destiny imply determinism, and thus a crucial loss of freedom. If there is a plurality of times, or if time is cyclic, then prophecy and destiny can coexist with a freedom of choice.

Perhaps at the beginning
time and the visible,
twin makers of distance,
arrived together,
drunk
battering on the door
just before dawn.

The first light sobered them,
and examining the day,
they spoke
of the far, the past, the invisible.
They spoke of the horizons
surrounding everything
which had not yet disappeared.

"For Dante time is the content of history felt as a single synchronic act. And inversely the purpose of history is to keep time together so that all are brothers and companions in the same quest and conquest of time." (Osip Mandel'shtam)

Of all that has been inherited from the nineteenth century only certain axioms about time have passed largely unquestioned. The Left and Right, evolutionists, physicists, and most revolutionaries, all accept—at least on an historical scale —the nineteenth-century view of a unilinear and uniform "flow" of time.

Yet the notion of a uniform time, within which all events can be temporally related, depends upon the synthesizing capacity of a mind. Galaxies and particles in themselves propose nothing. There is a phenomenological problem at the start. One is obliged to begin with conscious experience.

Despite clocks and the regular turning of the earth, time is experienced as passing at different rates. This impression is generally dismissed as subjective, because time, according to the nineteenth-century view, is objective, incontestable, and indifferent; to its indifference there are no limits.

Yet perhaps our experience should not be dismissed so quickly. Supposing one accepts the clocks; time does not slow down or accelerate. But time appears to pass at different rates because our experience of its passing involves not a single but two dynamic processes which are opposed to each other: as accumulation and dissipation.

The deeper the experience of a moment, the greater the accumulation of experience. This is why the moment is lived as longer. The dissipation of the time-flow is checked. The lived durée is not a question of length but of depth or density. Proust understood this.

Yet it is not only a cultural truth. A natural equivalent to the periodic increase of the density of lived time can be found in those days of alternating sun and rain, in the spring or early summer, when plants grow, almost visibly, several millimeters or centimeters a day. These hours of spectacular growth and accumulation are *incommensurate* with the winter hours when the seed lies inert in the earth.

The content of time, that which time carries, seems to entail another dimension. Whether one calls this dimension the fourth, the fifth, or even (in relation to time) the third, is unimportant, and only depends upon the space/time model one is using. What matters is that this dimension is intractable to the regular, uniform flow of time. There may be a sense in which time does not sweep all before it. To assert that it did was a specifically nineteenth-century article of faith.

Earlier, the intractable dimension was allowed for. It is present in all cyclic views of time. In those days time passed, time went on, and it did so by turning on itself like a wheel. Yet for a wheel to turn there needs to be a surface like the ground which resists, which offers friction. It was against this resistance that the wheel turned. Cyclic views of time are based on a model whereby two forces are in play: a force (time) moving in one direction, and a force resisting that movement.

The body ages. The body is preparing to die. No theory of time offers a reprieve here. Death and time were always in alliance. Time took away more or less slowly: death more or less suddenly.

Earlier, however, death was also thought of as the companion of life, as the precondition for that which came into Being from Non-being; one was not possible without the other. As a result, death was qualified by that which it could not destroy or by that which would return.

That life is brief was continually lamented. Time was death's agent and one of life's constituents. But the timeless —that which death could not destroy—was another. All cyclic views of time held these two constituents together: the wheel turning and the ground on which it turned.

The mainstream of modern thought has removed time from this unity and transformed it into a single, all-powerful and active force. In so doing it has transferred the spectral character of death to the notion of time itself. Time has become Death triumphant over all.

To measure modern astronomic distances, one uses as a unit that distance which light will travel in one year. The magnitude of these distances, the degree of separation which they imply, seem almost boundless; the magnitude and the degree escape everything except pure calculation and even this calculation has the quality of an explosion. Yet, hidden within the conceptual system that allows man to measure and conceive of such boundlessness is the cyclic and local unit of the year, a unit which can be recognized because of its permanency, its repetition, and its local consistency. The calculation returns from the astronomic to the local, like a prodigal son.

This weakness of the mind, this homesickness which cannot or will not altogether abandon the here-and-now, can be interpreted in two ways. It can be seen as the revealing weakness which proves how lost and impotent man is in the universe; or it can be seen as the vestige, preserved by the structure of the human mind, of the original truth.

Pascal in the seventeenth century recognized the extent of the unprecedented rupture caused by the new calculations. With the advance of remorseless time and space, the past becomes lost and falls into nothingness. (The word *néant* is used in this absolute sense for the first time in the seventeenth century.) God abandons life, to inhabit the eternal domain of death. No longer present within the cycles of time, no longer the hub of these cycles, he becomes an absent, waiting presence. All the calculations underline how long he has already waited or will wait. The proofs of his existence cease to be the morning, the returning season, the newborn; instead they become the "eternity" of heaven and hell and the finality of the last judgment. Man now becomes condemned to time, which is no longer a condition of life and therefore something sacred, but the inhuman principle which spares nothing. Time becomes both a sentence and a punishment.

Henceforth only somebody reprieved from a death sentence can imagine time as a gift. And Pascal's famous wager —God may not exist, we may be lost, but supposing he does exist . . . —is a stratagem for imposing this death sentence and then hoping for a reprieve.

The modern era of quantification begins with algebra and infinite series. It follows that one no longer counts what one has, but what one has not. Everything becomes loss.

The concept of entropy is the figure of Death translated into a scientific principle. Yet whereas death used to be thought of as being the condition of life, entropy, it is maintained, will eventually exhaust and extinguish, not only lives, but life itself. And entropy, as Eddington termed it, "is time's arrow."

The modern transformation of time from a condition into a force began with Hegel. For Hegel, however, the force of history was positive; there has rarely been a more optimistic philosopher. Later Marx set out to prove that this force—the force of history—was subject to man's actions and choices. The always present drama in Marx's thinking, the original opposition of his dialectics, stems from the fact that he both accepted the modern transformation of time into the supreme force, and wished to return this supremacy into the hands of man. This is why his thought was—in all senses of the word —gigantic. The size of man—his potential, his coming power—would, Marx believed, replace the timeless.

Today, in the West, as the culture of capitalism abandons its claim to be a culture and becomes nothing more than an Instant-Practice, the force of time is pictured as the supreme and unopposed annihilator. The planet Earth and the universe are running down. Disorder increases with every time unit that passes. The final state of maximum entropy, where there will be no activity at all, is termed heat-death.

To question the finality of the principle of entropy is not to dispute the second law of thermodynamics. Within a given system, this and the other laws of thermodynamics can apply to what unfolds within time. They are laws of time's processes. It is their finality which can be disputed.

The process of increasing entropy ends with heat-death. It began with a state of maximum energy, which in astrophysical terms is thought of as an explosion. The theory necessitates a beginning and an end; both these face on to what is beyond time. The theory of entropy ultimately treats time as a parenthesis, and yet has nothing to say, and has eliminated everything that might be said, about what precedes or follows the parenthesis. Therein lies its innocence.

Many previous cosmological explanations of the world proposed, as does the theory of entropy, an ideal original state and afterwards, for man, a continually deteriorating situation. The Golden Age, the Garden of Eden, the Time of the Gods . . . all were far away from the misery of the present.

That life may be seen as a Fall is intrinsic to the human faculty of imagination. To imagine is to conceive of that height from which the Fall becomes possible.

The Adams and Eves
continually expelled
and with what tenacity
returning at night!

Before,
when the two of them
did not count
and there were no months

no births and no music
their fingers were unnumbered.

Before,
when the two of them did not count
did they feel
a prickling behind the eyes
a thirst in the throat
for something other than
the perfume of infinite flowers
and the breath of immortal animals?
In their untrembling sleep
did the tips of their tongues
seek the bud of another taste
which was mortal and sweating?

Did they envy the longing
of those to come after the Fall?

Women and men still return
to live through the night
all that uncounted time.

And with the punctuality
of the first firing squad
the expulsion is at dawn.

If there were no process of aging, if time and its passing
were not built into the very code of life, reproduction would
be unnecessary and sexuality would not exist. That sexuality

is a species leap over death has always been clear; it is one of the truths which precede philosophy.

Love insists upon making a comparable leap over death but, by definition, it cannot be a species leap, because the beloved constitutes the most particular and differentiated image of which the human imagination is capable. Every hair of your head.

The sexual thrust to reproduce and to fill the future is a thrust against the current of time which is flowing ceaselessly towards the past. The genetic information which assures reproduction works against dissipation. The sexual animal— like a grain of corn—is a conduit of the past into the future. The scale of that span over millennia, and the distance covered by that temporal short circuit which is fertilization, are such that sexuality—even for women and men—is impersonal. The message dwarfs the messenger. The impersonal force of sexuality opposes the impersonal passing of time and is antithetical to it.

Every life is both created by, and held in, the encounter of these two opposing forces. To speak of such "holding" is another way of defining Being. What is so baffling and mysterious about Being is that it represents both stillness and movement. The stillness of an equilibrium created by the movement of two opposing forces.

The force of sexuality is forever unfinished, is never completed. Or, rather, it finishes only to re-begin, as if for the first time.

Differently, the ideal of love is to contain all. "Here I understand," wrote Camus, "what they call glory: the right to love without limits." This limitlessness is not passive, for the totality which love continually reclaims is precisely the totality which time appears to fragment and hide. Love is a reconstitution in the heart of that holding which is Being.

ONCE IN A SONG

A singer may be innocent
never the song. With its instantaneous eyes
opened on to the world
and its heart laid bare,
the song is brazen,
the song is newborn.
Only when it has quietened
can listeners resume by habit
the innocence of their age.

When a great singer sings, the skin of space and of time go
taut, the voices of the newborn fill the world, there is no
corner left of silence or of innocence, the gown of life is
turned inside out, the singer becomes earth and sky, time past
and time to come are singing one of the songs of a single
life.

Age. Date and place of birth.
Permanent address.
Date of entry into the country

ONCE IN THE HIGHLANDS

The crofters' cottages crouch like animals sheltering on the ground for the night. Everything moves on, the larches, the bracken, the caledonian pines, the heather, the juniper bushes, the scrap grass. And then moving into the land, water: the rivers running to the sea, the sea with its tides filling lochs. And across both land and water the wind. And, above all, the northwest wind. The honking of the wild geese in the sky is like a fleeting measure, a counting in another algebra, of all this movement.

There are castles, there are lines which could be and have been defended, deaths, but there are no final barriers. This is why herring can be fished from water surrounded by brackened hills. This is why the sky can appear to have more flesh on it, to be more hospitable, than the land. Here between the land and sky it is like a shore. And as the seashore smells of seaweed, so this shore smells of uncounted time.

The uncounted time is heavy with a sense of loss. The Highlands lament those who have disappeared, supremely those who were forced to disappear. The number of those chased from the land during the clearances enters the inconsolable algebra of the geese.

Among the first islands off the western coast is Gigha. Five hundred years ago on its southern tip the islanders built a small chapel. It stood for three centuries and then fell into ruin. Around the chapel is a cemetery. The tombstones are not very different from those in other European cemeteries. Many record the deaths of several generations: the name, the year of birth, the day of death and the place of death, if it was not on the island. A name and two dates, the last one precise to the very day. This is what is recorded. About what happened between, apart from the bare fact of survival, not a word is written.

Salt, rain, lichen, and the wind efface the deepest-cut letters within a century or two. Why inscribe even the name and the two dates? The same question might be asked in any cemetery, but here, on the island, the answer is more evident.

The inscriptions are not for the living. Those who remembered the dead had no need to be reminded. What is inscribed is a form of identification and the identifications are addressed to a third party. The tombstones are letters of recommendation to the dead, concerning the newly departed, written in the hope that they, who have left, will not need to be renamed.

From the cemetery you and I looked across the straits, to the sea, to the sky above the sea and, far away, to the brackened mountains. The coastline there is sloped like the passage for a birth outwards—towards the open Atlantic. To this birthplace the nomadic dead travel. They are within speaking distance. The living do not know how to speak their language. Our stories are not read by the dead.

On your island
does the night fall later?
Am I walking a little ahead of you
so that no snake will bite
your sandalled foot?

The balance is never made.
This is why the stars are silent
offering no account.

How to measure
a season
against
the calendar of your absence?

How to measure
the stream
of my tangled light
in the mountain
of what has been
and will be?

The balance is never made.

Yet in the night your eyes and mine
sounding one another
show no trace of vertigo.

2/Here

DISTANCE

You have filled the thermos with coffee
packed our footprints if needed
to throw into the jaws
   of the untestifying
      eternal snow.

Together as carpenters with hammers
we have taught the distance
how to build a roof
   from the trees
      we run between.

In the silence behind
we no more hear the faraway
question of the summer house:
   And tomorrow where
      shall we go?

At dusk the harnessed dogs fear
there is no end to the forest.
And each night in the snow
   we calm them
      with our surprising laughter.

The visible has been and still remains the principal human source of information about the world. Through the visible one orientates oneself. Even perceptions coming from other senses are often translated into visual terms. (Vertigo is a pathological example: originating in the ear, one experiences it as a visual, spatial confusion.) It is thanks to the visible that one recognizes space as the precondition for physical existence. The visible brings the world to us. But at the same time it reminds us ceaselessly that it is a world in which we risk to be lost. The visible with its space also takes the world away from us. Nothing is more two-faced.

The visible implies an eye. It is the stuff of the relation between seen and seer. Yet the seer, when human, is conscious of what his eye cannot and will never see because of time and distance. The visible both includes him (because he sees) and excludes him (because he is not omnipresent). The visible consists for him of the seen which, even when it is threatening, confirms his existence, and of the unseen which defies that existence. The desire to *have seen*—the ocean, the desert, the aurora borealis—has a deep ontological basis.

To this human ambiguity of the visible one then has to add the visual experience of absence, whereby we no longer see what we saw. We face a *dis*appearance. And a struggle ensues to prevent what has disappeared, what has become invisible, falling into the negation of the unseen, defying our existence. Thus, the visible produces faith in the reality of the invisible and provokes the development of an inner eye which retains and assembles and arranges, as if in an interior, as if what has been seen may be forever partly protected against the ambush of space, which is absence.

Both life itself and the visible owe their existence to light. Before there was life, nothing was seen—unless by God. Neither the optical explanation of visual perception nor the evolutionist theory of the slow, hazardous development of the eye in response to the stimulus of light—neither of these dissolve the enigma which surrounds the fact that, at a certain moment, the visible was born, at a certain moment appearances were revealed as appearances. As a response to this enigma, the first faculty accredited to the most important gods was that of sight: an eye, often an all-seeing eye. Then it could be said: *The visible exists because it has already been seen.*

The Genesis story is consistent with this. The first thing God created was light. After every subsequent act of creation, the light allowed him to see that what he had created was good. At the end of the sixth day he *saw* everything that he had made and, *behold*, it was very good.

The Genesis story acknowledges the mystery of the visible's coming into being. This mystery is sustained and repeated in the universal experience of what has come to be called natural beauty. Whatever normative categories are employed, such beauty is always experienced as a form of revelation. It is felt to speak.

A waterfall is a waterfall is a waterfall. Its appearance and significance, look and meaning, become identical, whereas usually they are separate and have to be brought together by the one who is looking and questioning. Beauty's revelation is this fusion. Such a fusion changes one's spatial sense, or, rather, changes one's sense of Being in space.

The boundlessly visible includes but also excludes man. He sees, and he sees that he is being continually abandoned. Appearances belong to the boundless space of the visible. With his inner eye man experiences the space of his own imagination and reflection. Normally it is within the protection of this inner space that he places, retains, cultivates, lets run wild or constructs Meaning.

At the moment of revelation when appearance and meaning become identical, the space of physics and the seer's inner space coincide: momentarily and exceptionally the seer achieves an equality with the visible. To lose all sense of exclusion; to be at the center.

The post office was large and I suspect that its director was either inefficient or vicious; there was something demoralized about the staff behind the counter, as if unnecessary absurdities had been added to their burden of overwork.

There was invariably a long queue for the Poste Restante, probably because it was a frontier town. Sometimes there was one letter from you, sometimes several. For each letter I paid the price of half a loaf of bread.

The austerity of the large hall—the post office was built in the 1930s—must once have been thought of as a civic virtue, just as its spaciousness had been conceived as an expression of social hope. Now it looked bare, run-down, faceless.

Most of the staff were women of about your age. When I saw your handwriting on the envelope, which the woman behind the counter was still holding in her hand, I heard your voice. Hearing it was not like remembering it. To remember is to recall. There in the central post office, with its imitation marble floor that amplified every footstep and shuffle—it was I who was called.

A voice belongs first to a body, then to a language. The language may change but the voice stays the same. I recognize your voice before I know in what language you are speaking. In the post office you pronounced the name you had written on the envelope, yet it was not the two words which I heard, it was your voice.

It coexisted, your voice, with all the other events of the same moment: the Tunisian trying to phone his family in Djebeniana, the woman coming to fetch her mail-order parcel, the office clerk posting a hundred letters, the old man drawing his pension.

Perhaps it did not have to travel far; the distance between your voice and my ear was infinitesimal. But reality should never be confused with scale, it is only scale that has degrees.

The larger is *not* more real—if we tend to believe it is, the tendency is perhaps a vestige of the fear reflex to be found in all animals, in face of another creature larger than themselves. It is more prudent to believe that the large is more real than the small. Yet it is false. In death it is scale that falls apart; just as, at conception, a point fuses with the universe to create scale. If we are trapped, my heart, it is not within reality.

Perhaps lilac is the most abundantly feminine of flowers. It came from Eastern Europe and was imported into the West in the sixteenth century. A Slav flower.

Among the mountains here, the lilac trees flower at the time when the first cuckoos sing. Cuckoos and lilac come as a pair. The cuckoo is pure impudence. Later when he falls silent after mating, he eats grubs and caterpillars—even those which are poisonous for other birds—with impunity.

The scent of lilac, you once said, is not so far from the

smell of cows in the stable. Both are smells of peace and procrastination.

The days are becoming long, and in the evening I sit in the kitchen reading without a light. On the windowsill is a jug with a flowering branch of lilac, which I cut in a friend's garden. It is pale purple, the color of a much-washed ultramarine blue shirt. When I was young, I had a shirt of that color, and the great Indonesian painter, Affandi, painted a portrait of me in it. Both portrait and shirt have disappeared. Through the open window I can hear a cuckoo, and the chain saws of the woodcutters still working.

When I glanced up a moment ago, the branch of lilac in the fading light looked like a distant hill of blossoming trees merging into the dusk. It was disappearing.

The walls of the house are thick, for the winters are cold. On the window embrasure, close to the windowpanes, hangs a shaving mirror. As I look up now, I see reflected in the mirror a sprig of the lilac branch: each petal of each tiny flower is vivid, distinct, near, so near that the petals look like the pores of a skin. At first I do not understand why what I see in the mirror is so much more intense than the rest of the branch which, in fact, is nearer to me. Then I realize that what I am looking at in the mirror is the *far* side of the lilac, the side fully lit by the last light of the sun.

Every evening my love for you is placed like that mirror.

"Philosophy is really homesickness, it is the urge to be at home everywhere."—Novalis

The transition from a nomadic life to a settled one is said to mark the beginning of what was later called civilization.

Soon all those who survived outside the city began to be considered uncivilized. But that is another story—to be told in the hills near the wolves.

Perhaps during the last century and a half an equally important transformation has taken place. Never before our time have so many people been uprooted. Emigration, forced or chosen, across national frontiers or from village to metropolis, is the quintessential experience of our time. That industrialization and capitalism would require such a transport of men on an unprecedented scale and with a new kind of violence was already prophesied by the opening of the slave trade in the sixteenth century. The Western Front in the First World War with its conscripted massed armies was a later confirmation of the same practice of tearing up, assembling, transporting and concentrating in a "no-man's-land." Later, concentration camps, across the world, followed the logic of the same continuous practice.

All the modern historians from Marx to Spengler have identified the contemporary phenomenon of emigration. Why add more words? To whisper for that which has been lost. Not out of nostalgia, but because it is on the site of loss that hopes are born.

The term *home* (Old Norse *Heimr*, High German *heim*, Greek *kōmi*, meaning "village") has, since a long time, been taken over by two kinds of moralists, both dear to those who wield power. The notion of *home* became the keystone for a code of domestic morality, safeguarding the property (which included the women) of the family. Simultaneously the notion of *homeland* supplied a first article of faith for patriotism, persuading men to die in wars which often served no other interest except that of a minority of their ruling class. Both usages have hidden the original meaning.

Originally home meant the center of the world—not in a geographical, but in an ontological sense. Mircea Eliade has

[55]

demonstrated how home was the place from which the world could be *founded*. A home was established, as he says, "at the heart of the real." In traditional societies, everything that made sense of the world was real; the surrounding chaos existed and was threatening, but it was threatening because it was *unreal*. Without a home at the center of the real, one was not only shelterless, but also lost in non-being, in unreality. Without a home everything was fragmentation.

Home was the center of the world because it was the place where a vertical line crossed with a horizontal one. The vertical line was a path leading upwards to the sky and downwards to the underworld. The horizontal line represented the traffic of the world, all the possible roads leading across the earth to other places. Thus, at home, one was nearest to the gods in the sky and to the dead in the underworld. This nearness promised access to both. And at the same time, one was at the starting point and, hopefully, the returning point of all terrestrial journeys.

The crossing of the two lines, the reassurance their intersection promises, was probably already there, in embryo, in the thinking and beliefs of nomadic people, but they carried the vertical line with them, as they might carry a tent pole. Perhaps at the end of this century of unprecedented transportation, vestiges of the reassurance still remain in the unarticulated feelings of many millions of displaced people.

Emigration does not only involve leaving behind, crossing water, living amongst strangers, but, also, undoing the very meaning of the world and—at its most extreme—abandoning oneself to the unreal which is the absurd.

Emigration, when it is not enforced at gunpoint, may of course be prompted by hope as well as desperation. For example, to the peasant son the father's traditional authority may seem more oppressively absurd than any chaos. The poverty of the village may appear more absurd than the crimes of the metropolis. To live and die amongst foreigners may seem less absurd than to live persecuted or tortured by one's fellow countrymen. All this can be true. But to emigrate is always to dismantle the center of the world, and so to move into a lost, disoriented one of fragments.

8 POEMS OF EMIGRATION

1. Village

I tell you
    all houses
are holes in an arse of stone

we eat off coffin lids

between evening star
    and milk in a bucket
is nothing

the churn is emptied
    twice a day

cast us
    steaming
        on the fields.

2. *Earth*

the purple scalp of the earth
combed in autumn
     and times of famine

the metal bones of the earth
     extracted by hand

the church above the earth
     arms of our clock crucified

all is taken

3. *Leaving*

pain
cannot

endure long enough

tracks vanish
under snow
the white embrace
of leaving

I have tried to write the truth on trains

without an ear
the tongue takes fright
clings to a single word

the train is crossing a bridge
black ice collects
on each letter
S A V A
my river

4. *Metropolis*

the edge of moonlight
sharp
like the level
    of water in a canal

and the locks of reason
at dawn
when the level of the dark
is brought down
    to that of the light

accept the dark
massed black
zone of blindness
accept it eyes

but here the dark
has been stolen in a sack
weighted down with a pebble
and drowned

there is no longer any dark

5. Factory

here
it is dawn eternally
hour of awakening
hour of revolutionary prophecy
hour of the embers dead
time of the days work
without end

there we built the night
as we lit the fire
lay down in it
pulled up the dark as blanket

near fields were
the breath of animals asleep
quiet as the earth
warm as the fire

cold is the pain of believing
warmth will never return

here
night is time forgotten
eternal dawn
and in the cold I dream
    of how the pine
    burnt
    like a dog's tongue
    behind its teeth

6. Waterfront

all night Hudson
coughs in bed

I try to sleep

my country
is a hide nailed to wood

the wind of my soul rushes

out of horizons
I make a hammock

in sleep
I suck birth village
touch my river's curve

two black mackerel
pilot in
daybreak

gaff them sky gaff them

7. Absence

when the sun was no higher than the grass
jewels hung in the trees
and the terraces turned rose
between fluorescent lights along the ringroad
apartments hang their pietàs

they are frying potatoes
a factory discharges its hands in woollen gloves
there is a hole in my thumb

the vines are not green
the vines are not here
the jewels
crushed in high voltage wires
will be worn by the dead
DANGER DE MORT

8. *A Forest I Knew*

let me die like this

the branches have muscles
    hills get up
the cloud pours
    into a cup

in the forest wild boar
    have eaten
    are warm
       and sleepy

each clearing is recorded
    on a screen I carry
rolled like a cloth
    in my head

              a sheet
                  pulled over
                       the eyes of the dead
              keeps out the look of the world
              on the cloth
                  unrolled
              I follow their spoor
                  in the forest I knew.

Baudelaire was among the first to name and describe the
homelessness of the new city crowds.
              ". . . . like errant homeless ghosts
                  doggedly bemoaning."
Yet the judgment—not the poetry—is too sweeping. The
very sense of loss keeps alive an expectation. How easy it is to
lose sight of what is historically invisible—as if people lived
only history and nothing else!

Popular ingenuity is often invisible. Occasionally, when
gathered into political action, it becomes visible. The rest of
the time it is used daily for clandestine personal survival. At
the practical level of dodging, picking up, hustling: and at the
psychic level of turning in circles in order to preserve one's
identity. The masses, the required anonymous labor force,
persist in remaining a population of individuals, despite their
living and working conditions, despite their displacement.
And the ground of each one of these preserved individualities
is like a home.

The "substitute" home has little to do with a building.
The roof over the head, the four walls, have become, as it
were, secular: independent from whatever is kept in the heart
and is sacred. Such secularization is the direct consequence of
economic and social conditions: tenancy, poverty, over-

crowding, city planning, property speculation. But ultimately it is the consequence of a lack of choice. Without a history of choice no dwelling can be a home.

With the traditional dwelling which was a home, the choice may have been ancestral, even beyond living memory, but every act of maintenance or improvement acknowledged and repeated the first choice, which was not one of taste but of *insight*, in having chosen a place where the two life lines crossed. The choices open to women and men today—even amongst the underprivileged—may be more numerous than in the past, but what has been lost irretrievably is the choice of saying: this is the center of the world.

Nevertheless, by turning in circles the displaced preserve their identity and improvise a shelter. Built of what? Of habits, I think, of the raw material of repetition, turned into a shelter. The habits imply words, jokes, opinions, gestures, actions, even the way one wears a hat. Physical objects and places—a piece of furniture, a bed, the corner of a room, a particular bar, a street corner—supply the scene, the site of the habit, yet it is not they but the habit which protects. The mortar which holds the improvised "home" together—even for a child—is memory. Within it, visible, tangible mementoes are arranged—photos, trophies, souvenirs—but the roof and four walls which safeguard the lives within, these are invisible, intangible, and biographical.

To the underprivileged, home is represented, not by a house, but by a practice or set of practices. Everyone has his own. These practices, chosen and not imposed, offer in their repetition, transient as they may be in themselves, more permanence, more shelter than any lodging. Home is no longer a dwelling but the untold story of a life being lived. At its most brutal, home is no more than one's name—whilst to most people one is nameless.

[6 4]

The sky is blue black
starlings unfold their wings
quit their pediments
to write a letter
returned.
The setting sun
fills teeth with gold.
Like a shred of meat
I'm lodged in this town.

The experience of newly arrived immigrants is different
from that of a long established, "indigenous" proletariat or
sub-proletariat. Yet the displacement, the homelessness, the
abandonment lived by a migrant is the extreme form of a
more general and widespread experience. The term "aliena-
tion" confesses all. (It would even be possible to talk of the
"homelessness" of the bourgeois with his town house, his
country house, his three cars, his several televisions, his tennis
court, his wine cellar—it would be just possible, yet nothing
about his class now interests me, for there is nothing left to discover there for the future.)

After the migrant leaves home, he never finds another
place where the two life lines cross. The vertical line exists no
more; there is no longer any local continuity between him
and the dead, the dead now simply disappear; and the gods
have become inaccessible. The vertical line has been twisted
into the individual biographical circle which leads nowhere
but only encloses. As for the horizontal lines, because there
are no longer any fixed points as bearings, they are elided

into a plain of pure distance, across which everything is swept.

What can grow on this site of loss? Perhaps it can only be that which, earlier, when every village was the center of the world, remained inconceivable. Since the beginning of the nineteenth century, at least two new expectations—offering the hope of a new shelter—have become more and more widely shared.

The first is that of passionate romantic love. (Of which there is more in the backstreets than in the libraries.) In one sense what happens between women and men in love is beyond history. In the fields, on the roads, in the workshops, at school, there are continual transformations: in an embrace very little changes. Yet the construction put on passion alters. Not necessarily because emotions are different but because what surrounds the emotions—social attitudes, legal systems, moralities, eschatologies—these change.

Romantic love, in the modern sense, is a love uniting or hoping to unite two displaced persons. Friendship, solidarity, mutual interests can also unite people, but they do so according to experience and circumstances. They usually have an empirical basis. Whereas romantic love remembers beginnings and origins. Its primacy pre-dates experience. And it is this primacy which allows it to have a special meaning (from Novalis to Frank Sinatra) in the modern epoch.

In the beginning, which such love remembers, the division into two sexes polarized life. The creation of male and female constituted a separation, a new form of incompleteness. The sexual instinct was the energy of attraction between the two poles. As soon as human imagination and memory existed, the desire to hold and maintain that attraction began to declare itself as love. Such love held out a hope of completion, and proposed that its own energy belonged to the heart of the real. The hope of completion developed simultaneously with the founding of the home, but it was not the same thing.

In the modern period when we are deprived of the second, we feel more intensely than ever before the resonance of the first.

The other expectation is historical. Every migrant knows in his heart of hearts that it is impossible to return. Even if he is physically able to return, he does not truly return, because he himself has been so deeply changed by his emigration. It is equally impossible to return to that historical state in which every village was the center of the world. The one hope of re-creating a center now is to make it the entire earth. Only worldwide solidarity can transcend modern homelessness. Fraternity is too easy a term; forgetting Cain and Abel, it somehow promises that all problems can be soluble. In reality many are insoluble—hence the never-ending need for solidarity.

Today, as soon as very early childhood is over, the house can never again be home, as it was in other epochs. This century, for all its wealth and with all its communication systems, is the century of banishment. Eventually perhaps the promise, of which Marx was the great prophet, will be fulfilled, and then the substitute for the shelter of a home will not just be our personal names, but our collective conscious presence in history, and we will live again at the heart of the real. Despite everything, I can imagine it.

Meanwhile, we live not just our own lives but the longings of our century.

TWENTIETH CENTURY STORM

Lightning the scythe
is cutting down the rain.
Swathes of water

fall like the clothes
—o the great coats for parting
   the great great coats
   that never returned!
fall like the clothes
of the far away
on the sky's empty field.

And in the grass of this rain
flowers
which grew with the strength of rivers
—o the pockets of the ferryman
   packed with the letters
   silences and promised numbers
   of those who left!
which grew with the strength of rivers
into estuaries.

Each flower began
in the palm of a hand,
each petal
in origin
a gesture an action
a touching.

Put your garden to my cheek
your five fingered garden
in another city
to my cheek.

The haycart
loaded with thunder
is trundling across the sky

The existence of pleasure is the first mystery. The existence of pain has prompted far more philosophical speculation. Pleasure and pain need to be considered together, they are inseparable. Yet the space filled by each is perhaps different.

Pleasure, defined as a sense of gratification, is essential for nature's workings. Otherwise there would be no impulse to satisfy the needs which ensure the body's and the species' survival. And survival—for reasons we do not know—is inwritten, inscribed as nature's only goal. Gratification, or its anticipation, acts as a goad. Pain or the fear of pain acts as a warning. Both are essential. The difference between them, considered as opposites, is that pleasure has a constant tendency to exceed its functional purpose, *to not know its place.*

Cats display more pleasure when licking one another than when eating. (There is, it is true, in all animals, except ruminants, an urgency in eating which displaces pleasure: the pleasure comes as plenitude after the act of eating.) Horses running wild in a field appear to experience more pleasure than when quenching their thirst. The gratification, necessary in order to provoke impulses towards the satisfaction of certain essential needs, produces, even in animals, a capacity for a generalized experience of pleasure. Gratuitous pleasure.

Perhaps this capacity is linked to the fact that all young animals need to play in order to learn. Between play and gratuitous pleasure there is a face in common. Playing implies a distinction between the real and the playful. The world is doubled by play. There is the involuntary world of necessity and the voluntary world of play. In the second world pleasure no longer serves a purpose but becomes gratuitous.

For us too, the world is doubled by play, but the degree of invention mounts so that play becomes imagination. Imagination doubles and intensifies both pain and pleasure: anxiety and fantasy are born. Nevertheless the same elementary distinction remains. Pain, however much it overflows its source, always has a cause, a center, a locus; whereas pleasure does not necessarily have one.

Human happiness is rare. There are no happy periods, only happy moments. But happiness is precisely a generalized pleasure. And the state of happiness can be defined by an equation whereby, at that moment, the gift of one's well-being equals the gift of the existent. Without a surplus of pleasure over and above functional gratification, such well-being could not exist. Aesthetic experience is the purest expression of this equation.

Traditionally this equation was read as the sign of the existence of a benevolent God or, at least, of a God sometimes capable of benevolence. The arbitrariness of happiness was interpreted as a divine intention. And from this arose the problem of suffering and pain. If pleasure was a gift, if happiness was intended, why should there be pain? The answers are hard.

It has never been easy to relieve pain. The productive recourses have usually been lacking—food, adequate medicines, clothing, shelter. But it has never been difficult to locate the causes of pain: hunger, illness, cold, deprivation. . . . It has always been, in principle, simpler to relieve pain than to give pleasure or make happy. An area of pain is more easily located.

With one enormous exception—the emotional pain of loss, the pain that has broken a heart. Such pain fills the space of an entire life. It may have begun with a single event but the event has produced a surplus of pain. The sufferer becomes inconsolable. Yet, what is this pain, if it is not the recognition that what was once given as pleasure or happiness has been irrevocably taken away?

The gift of pleasure is the first mystery.

A LOVE SONG

The mountains are pitiless
the rain is melting the snow
it will freeze again.

In the café two strangers
play the accordion
and a roomful of men are singing.

Tunes are filling
the sacks of the heart
the troughs of eyes.

Words are filling
the stalls
which bellow between the ears.

Music shaves the jowls
loosens the joints,
the only cure for rheumatism.

Music cleans the nails
softens the hands
scours the calluses.

A roomful of men,
come from drenched cattle
diesel oil, the eternal shovel,

are caressing
the air of a love song
with sweetened hands.

Mine have left my wrists
and are crossing the mountains
to find your breasts.

In the café two strangers
play the accordion
the rain is melting the snow.

For an animal its natural environment and habitat are a
given; for man—despite the faith of the empiricists—reality
is not a given: it has to be continually sought out, held—I am
tempted to say *salvaged.* One is taught to oppose the real to
the imaginary, as though the first were always at hand and the
second distant, far away. This opposition is false. Events are
always to hand. But the coherence of these events—which is
what one means by reality—is an imaginative construction.
Reality always *lies beyond*—and this is as true for ma-
terialists as for idealists. For Plato, for Marx. Reality, however one interprets it, lies beyond a screen of clichés. Every
culture produces such a screen, partly to facilitate its own

practices (to establish habits) and partly to consolidate its own power. Reality is inimical to those with power.

All modern artists have thought of their innovations as offering a closer approach to reality, as a way of making reality more evident. It is here, and only here, that the modern artist and revolutionary have sometimes found themselves side by side, both inspired by the idea of pulling down the screen of clichés, clichés which have increasingly become unprecedentedly trivial and egotistical.

Yet many such artists have reduced what they found beyond the screen, to suit their own talent and social position as artists. When this has happened they have justified themselves with one of the dozen variants of the theory of art for art's sake. They say: Reality is art. They hope to extract an artistic profit from reality. Of no one is this less true than Van Gogh.

One knows from his letters how intensely he was aware of the screen. His whole life story is one of an endless yearning for reality. Colors, the Mediterranean climate, the sun, were for him vehicles going towards this reality; they were never objects of longing in themselves. This yearning was intensified by the crises he suffered when he felt that he was failing to salvage any reality at all. Whether these crises are today diagnosed as being schizophrenic or epileptic, changes nothing; their content, as distinct from their pathology, was a vision of reality consuming itself like a phoenix.

One also knows from his letters that nothing appeared more sacred to him than work. He saw the physical reality of labor as being, simultaneously, a necessity, an injustice, and the essence of humanity throughout history. The artist's creative act was for him only one among many such acts. He believed that reality could best be approached through work, precisely because reality itself was a form of production.

His paintings speak of this more clearly than do words.

Their so-called clumsiness, the gestures with which he drew with pigment upon the canvas, the gestures (invisible today but imaginable) with which he chose and mixed his colors on the palette, all the gestures with which he handled and manufactured the stuff of the painted image, are analogous to the *activity* of the existence of what he is painting. His paintings imitate the active existence—the labor of being—of what they depict.

A chair, a bed, a pair of boots. His act of painting them was far nearer than that of any other painter to the carpenter's or the shoemaker's act of making them. He brings together the elements of the product—legs, crossbars, back, seat—sole, uppers, tongue, heel—as though he too were fitting them together, *joining* them, and as if this *being joined* constituted their reality.

Before a landscape this same process was far more complicated and mysterious, yet it followed the same principle. If one imagines God creating the world from earth and water, from clay, his way of handling it to make a tree or a cornfield might well resemble the way that Van Gogh handled paint when he painted a tree or cornfield. He was human, there was nothing divine about him. If, however, one thinks of the creation of the world, one can imagine the act only through the visual evidence, here and now, of the energy of the forces in play. And to these energies, Van Gogh was terribly attuned.

When he painted a small pear tree in flower, the act of the sap rising, of the bud forming, the bud breaking, the flower opening, the styles thrusting out, the stigmas becoming sticky, these acts were all present for him in the act of painting. When he painted a road, the roadmakers were there in his imagination. When he painted the turned earth of a ploughed field, the gesture of the blade turning the earth was included in his own act. Wherever he looked he saw the labor of existence; and this labor, recognized as such, was what constituted reality for him.

When he painted his own face, he painted the production of his destiny, past and future, rather as palmists believe they can read such a production in the lines of the hand. His contemporaries, who considered him abnormal, were not all as stupid as is now assumed. He painted compulsively—no other painter was ever compelled in a comparable way.

And his compulsion? It was to bring the two acts of production—that of the canvas and that of the reality depicted—ever closer and closer. This compulsion derived not from an idea about art—this is why it never occurred to him to profit from reality—but from an overwhelming feeling of empathy.

"I admire the bull, the eagle, and man with such an intense adoration, that it will certainly prevent me from ever becoming an ambitious person."

He was compelled to go ever closer, to approach and approach and approach. *In extremis* he approaches so close that the stars in the night sky became maelstroms of light, the cypress trees ganglions of living wood responding to the energy of wind and sun. There are canvases where reality dissolves him, the painter. But in hundreds of others he takes the spectator as close as any man can, while remaining intact, to that permanent process by which reality is being produced.

Once, long ago, paintings were compared with mirrors. Van Gogh's might be compared with lasers. They do not wait to receive, they go out to meet, and what they traverse is, not so much empty space, as the act of production, the production of the world. Painting after painting is a way of saying, with awe but little comfort: Dare to come this close and see how it works!

The silence after a felled tree has fallen is like the silence immediately after a death. The same sense of culmination. For a moment the tree's weight—which is all that still renders it a little dangerous—accords with the weight of the finished act.

The moment is exceedingly brief, for either fatigue—the daily fatigue of the woodcutter or the routine task of stripping the tree—quickly intervenes. Yet, just as the briefest glimpse of a full naked breast may recall the past to anyone, so the sight of the sudden stillness of a felled tree recalls death.

Even when working in the forest alone, one has an elusive sense of company. A flat field, a bare hillside, or the steppe are not the same. The trees constitute a presence. They maintain—each according to its species—an extraordinary balance between movement and stillness, between action and passivity. And in this balance, all the while being regulated, their presence is palpable. That they held up the roofs of houses for so long is not surprising. They offer company. But company of a discretion which is indistinguishable from indifference. They roofed not only houses but also courts, tax-collector's offices, prisons, armories.

Their presence, if it offers a kind of company, is earlier than justice or the notion of indifference. The company they offer is spatial, and it is a way of measuring, of counting. Long before any numerals or mathematics, when human language was first naming the world, trees offered their measures

—of distance, of height, of diameter, of space. They were taller than anything else alive, their roots went deeper than any creature; they grazed the sky and sounded the underworld. From them was born the idea of the pillar, the column. Trees offered man the measure of his upright space, and in this offer—mysteriously still present today as I fill up the chain saw with petrol—there is the discreetest assurance in the world, that we have never been utterly alone.

Each pine at dusk
lodges the bird
of its voice
perpendicular and still
the forest
indifferent to history
tearless as stone
repeats
in tremulous excitement
the ancient story
of the sun going down

At the end of the day when they come out of the forest, their limbs scarcely any longer obedient to their instructions, carrying their chain saws and bottles, the unfiltered light and the panorama dazzle their eyes. Each time they are astounded and, somewhere in the heavy oppressive fatigue of their bodies, there is almost a smile, as if in response to a wink. After hours of the forest, what is winking at them is the space of the valleys below and the unimpeded sky. Each pursues his own path down the slope, led by the weakness of his knees or by his boots that feel their way through the grass without him.

Each is going to his own rest. But they are all returning to the world, and its first gift is its space; later, its second gift will be a flat table and a bed. For the most fortunate the bed is shared.

Even after the great separation we shall return to you at the end of the day, out of the unimpeded sky, and you will recognize us by our fatigue and by the heaviness of our heads on your bodies, of which we had such need.

According to whether we are in the same place or separated one from the other, I know you twice. There are two of you.

When you are away, you are nevertheless present for me. This presence is multiform: it consists of countless images, passages, meanings, things known, landmarks, yet the whole remains marked by your absence, in that it is diffuse. It is as if your person becomes a place, your contours horizons. I live in you then like living in a country. You are everywhere. Yet in that country I can never meet you face to face.

Partir est mourir un peu. I was very young when I first heard this sentence quoted and it expressed a truth I already knew. I remember it now because the experience of living in you as if you were a country, the only country in the world where I can never conceivably meet you face to face, this is a little like the experience of living with the memory of the dead. What I did not know when I was very young was that nothing can take the past away: the past grows gradually around one, like a placenta for dying.

In the country which is you I know your gestures, the intonations of your voice, the shape of every part of your body. You are not physically less real there, but you are less free.

What changes when you are there before my eyes is that you become unpredictable. What you are about to do is unknown to me. I follow you. You act. And with what you do, I fall in love again.

One night in bed you asked me who was my favorite painter. I hesitated, searching for the least knowing, most truthful answer. Caravaggio. My own reply surprised me. There are nobler painters and painters of greater breadth of vision. There are painters I admire more and who are more admirable. But there is none, so it seems—for the answer came unpremeditated—to whom I feel closer.

The few canvases from my own incomparably modest life as a painter, which I would like to see again, are those I painted in the late 1940s of the streets of Livorno. This city was then war-scarred and poor, and it was there that I first began to learn something about the ingenuity of the dispossessed. It was there too that I discovered that I wanted as little as possible to do in this world with those who wield power. This has turned out to be a lifelong aversion.

The complicity I feel with Caravaggio began, I think, during that time in Livorno. He was the first painter of life as experienced by the popolaccio, the people of the backstreets, les sans-culottes, the lumpenproletariat, the lower orders, those of the lower depths, the underworld. There is no word in any traditional European language which does not either denigrate or patronize the urban poor it is naming. That is power.

Following Caravaggio up to the present day, other painters—Brower, Ostade, Hogarth, Goya, Géricault, Guttuso—have painted pictures of the same social milieu. But all of them—however great—were genre pictures, painted in order to show others how the less fortunate or the more dangerous lived. With Caravaggio, however, it was not a question of presenting scenes but of seeing itself. He does not depict the underworld for others: his vision is one that he shares with it.

In art-historical books Caravaggio is listed as one of the great innovating masters of chiaroscuro and a forerunner of the light and shade later used by Rembrandt and others. His vision can of course be considered art-historically as a step in the evolution of European art. Within such a perspective *a* Caravaggio was almost inevitable, as a link between the high art of the Counter Reformation and the domestic art of the emerging Dutch bourgeoisie, the form of this link being that of a new kind of space, defined by darkness as well as by light. (For Rome and for Amsterdam damnation had become an everyday affair.)

For the Caravaggio who actually existed—for the boy called Michelangelo born in a village near Bergamo, not far from where my friends, the Italian woodcutters, come—light and shade, as he imagined and saw them, had a deeply personal meaning, inextricably entwined with his desires and his instinct for survival. And it is by this, not by any art-historical logic, that his art is linked with the underworld.

His chiaroscuro allowed him to banish daylight. Shadows, he felt, offered shelter as can four walls and a roof. Whatever and wherever he painted he really painted interiors. Sometimes—for *The Flight into Egypt* or one of his beloved John the Baptists—he was obliged to include a landscape in the background. But these landscapes are like rugs or drapes hung up on a line across an inner courtyard. He only felt at home—no, that he felt nowhere—he only felt relatively at ease *inside*.

His darkness smells of candles, overripe melons, damp washing waiting to be hung out the next day: it is the darkness of stairwells, gambling corners, cheap lodgings, sudden encounters. And the promise is not in what will flare against it, but in the darkness itself. The shelter it offers is only relative, for the chiaroscuro reveals violence, suffering, longing, mortality, but at least it reveals them intimately. What has been banished, along with the daylight, are distance and solitude—and both these are feared by the underworld.

Those who live precariously and are habitually crowded together develop a phobia about open spaces which transforms their frustrating lack of space and privacy into something reassuring. He shared those fears.

The Calling of St. Matthew depicts five men sitting round their usual table, telling stories, gossiping, boasting of what one day they will do, counting money. The room is dimly lit. Suddenly the door is flung open. The two figures who enter are still part of the violent noise and light of the invasion. (Berenson wrote that Christ, who is one of the figures, comes in like a police inspector to make an arrest.)

Two of Matthew's colleagues refuse to look up, the other two younger ones stare at the strangers with a mixture of curiosity and condescension. Why is he proposing something so mad? Who's protecting him, the thin one who does all the talking? And Matthew, the tax-collector with a shifty conscience which has made him more unreasonable than most of his colleagues, points at himself and asks: Is it really I who must go? Is it really I who must follow you?

How many thousands of decisions to leave have resembled Christ's hand here! The hand is held out towards the one who has to decide, yet it is ungraspable because so fluid. It orders the way, yet offers no direct support. Matthew will get up and follow the thin stranger from the room, down the narrow streets, out of the district. He will write his gospel, he will travel to Ethiopa and the South Caspian and Persia. Probably he will be murdered.

And behind the drama of this moment of decision in the room at the top of the stairs, there is a window, giving onto the outside world. Traditionally in painting, windows were treated either as sources of light or as frames framing nature or framing an exemplary event outside. Not so this window. No light enters by it. The window is opaque. We see nothing. Mercifully we see nothing because what is outside is bound to be threatening. It is a window through which only the worst news can come.

Caravaggio was a heretical painter: his works were rejected or criticized by the Church because of their subject-matter, although certain Church figures defended him. His heresy consisted of transposing religious themes into popular tragedies. The fact that for *The Death of the Virgin* he reputedly took as a model a drowned prostitute is only half the story: the more important half is that the dead woman is laid out as the poor lay out their dead, and the mourners mourn her as the poor mourn. As the poor still mourn.

> There's no cemetery at Marinella or Selinunte, so when somebody dies we take him to the station and send him to Castelvetrano. Then us fishermen stick together. We pay our respects to the stricken family. "He was a good man. It's a real loss, he had lots of good years ahead of him." Then we go off to tend to our business in the port, but we never stop talking about the deceased and for three whole days we don't go out to fish. And close relatives or friends feed the mourners' families for at least a week.

Other Mannerist painters of the period produced turbulent crowd scenes but their spirit was very different; a crowd was seen as a sign of calamity—like fire or flood—and the mood was of terrestrial damnation. The spectator observed, from a privileged position, a cosmic theater. By contrast, Caravaggio's congested canvases are simply made up of individuals living cheek-by-jowl, coexisting in a confined space.

The underworld is full of theater, but one that has nothing to do with either cosmic effects or ruling-class entertainment. In the daily theater of the underworld everything is close-to and emphatic. What is being "played" may any moment become "for real." There is no protective space and no hierarchical focus of interest. Caravaggio was continually being criticized for exactly this—the lack of discrimination in his paintings, their overall intensity, their lack of a proper distance.

The underworld displays itself in hiding. This is the paradox of its social atmosphere and the expression of one of its deepest needs. It has its own heroes and villains, its own honor and dishonor, and these are celebrated by legends, stories, daily performances. The last are often somewhat like rehearsals for real exploits. They are scenes, created on the spur of the moment, in which people play themselves, pushed to the limit. If these "performances" did not take place, the alternative moral code and honor of the underworld would be in danger of being forgotten—or, to put it better, the negative judgment, the opprobrium of the surrounding society, would advance apace.

The underworld's survival and pride depend upon theater, a theater where everyone is flamboyantly playing and proving himself, and yet where an individual's survival may well depend on his lying low or his not being seen. The consequent tension produces a special kind of expressive urgency in which gestures fill all the space available, in which a life's desire may be expressed by a glance. This amounts to another kind of overcrowding, another kind of density.

Caravaggio is the painter of the underworld, and he is

also the exceptional and profound painter of sexual desire. Beside him most heterosexual painters look like pimps undressing their "ideals" for the spectator. He, though, had eyes only for the desired.

Desire changes its character by 180 degrees. Often, when first aroused, it is felt as the desire to have. The desire to touch is, partly, the desire to lay hands on, to take. Later, transformed, the same desire becomes a desire to be taken, to lose oneself within the desired. From these two opposed moments come one of the dialectics of desire; both moments apply to both sexes and they oscillate. Clearly the second moment, the desire to lose oneself within, is the most abandoned, the most desperate, and it is the one that Caravaggio chose (or was compelled) to reveal in many of his paintings.

The gestures of his figures are sometimes—given the nominal subject matter—ambiguously sexual. A six-year-old child fingers the Madonna's bodice; the Madonna's hand invisibly caresses his thigh under his shirt. An angel strokes the back of St. Matthew's evangelical hand like a prostitute with an elderly client. A young St. John the Baptist holds the foreleg of a sheep between his legs as if it were a penis.

Almost every act of touching which Caravaggio painted has a sexual charge. Even when two different substances (fur and skin, rags and hair, metal and blood) come into contact with one another, their contact becomes an act of touching. In his painting of a young boy as Cupid, the feather of one of the boy's wing tips touches his own upper thigh with a lover's precision. That the boy can control his reaction, that he does not allow himself to quiver in response, is part of his deliberate elusiveness, of his half-mocking, half-acknowledging practice as a seducer. I think of the marvelous Greek poet—Cavafy:

For a month we loved each other
Then he went away, I think to Smyrna,
To work there; we never saw each other again.

The grey eyes—if he lives—have lost their beauty;
The beautiful face will have been spoiled.

O Memory, preserve them as they were.
And, Memory, all you can of this love of mine
Whatever you can bring back to me tonight.

There is a special facial expression which, painted, exists
only in Caravaggio. It is the expression on Judith's face in
Judith and Holofernes, on the boy's face in the *Boy Being
Bitten by a Lizard*, on Narcissus's face as he gazes into the
water, on David's as he holds up the head of Goliath by the
giant's hair. It is an expression of closed concentration and
openness, of force and vulnerability, of determination and
pity. Yet all those words are too ethical. I have seen a not
dissimilar expression on the face of animals—before mating
and before a kill.

To think of it in sado-masochistic terms would be absurd.
It goes deeper than any personal predilection. If it vacillates,
this expression, between pleasure and pain, passion and re-
luctance, it is because such a dichotomy is inherent in sexual
experience itself. Sexuality is the result of an original unity
being destroyed, of separation. And, in this world as it is,
sexuality promises, as nothing else can, momentary completion. It touches a love to oppose the original cruelty.

The faces he painted are illuminated by that knowledge,
deep as a wound. They are the faces of the fallen—and they

offer themselves to desire with a truthfulness which only the fallen know to exist.

To lose oneself within the desired. How did Caravaggio express that in the way he painted bodies? Two young men, half dressed or undressed. Although young, their bodies bear the marks of use and experience. Soiled hands. A thigh already going to fat. Worn feet. A torso (with its nipple like an eye) which was born, grew up, sweats, pants, turns sleepless in the night—never a torso sculpted from an ideal. Not being innocent, their bodies contain experience.

And this means that their sentience can become palpable; on the other side of their skin is a universe. The flesh of the desired body is not a dreamt-of destination, but an immediate point of departure. Their very appearance beckons towards the *implicit*—in the most unfamiliar, carnal sense of that word. Caravaggio, painting them, dreams of their depths.

In Caravaggio's art, as one might expect, there is no property. A few tools and recipients, chairs and a table. And so around his figures there is little of interest. A body flares with light in an interior of darkness. The impersonal surroundings—like the world outside the window—can be forgotten. The desired body disclosed in the darkness, the darkness which is not a question of the time of day or night but of life as it is on this planet, the desired body, flaring like an apparition, beckons beyond—not by provocative gesture, but by the undisguised fact of its own sentience, promising the universe lying on the far side of its skin, calling you to leave. On the desired face an expression which goes further, much further, than invitation; for it is an acknowledgment of the self, of the cruelty of the world and of the one shelter, the one gift: to sleep together. Here. Now.

We with our vagrant language
we with our incorrigible accents
and another word for milk
we who come by train
and embrace on platforms
we and our wagons
we whose voice in our absence
is framed on a bedroom wall
we who share everything
and nothing—
this nothing which we break in two
and wash down with a gulp
from the only bottle,
we whom the cuckoo
taught to count,
into what currency
have they changed our singing?
What in our single beds
do we know of poetry?

We are experts in presents
both wrapped ones
and the others left surreptitiously.
Before leaving we hide our eyes our feet our backs.
What we take is for the luggage rack.
We leave our eyes behind
in the window frames and mirrors

our feet behind
on the carpet by the bed
our backs
in the mortar of the walls
and the doors hung on their hinges.
The door closed behind us
and the noise of the wagon wheels.

We are experts too in taking.
We take with us anniversaries
the shape of a fingernail
the silence of the child asleep
the taste of your celery
and the word for milk.
What in our single beds
do we know of poetry?

Single track, junction and
marshalling yards
read out loud to us.
No poem has longer lines
than those we have taken.
Like horsedealers we know how
to look a distance in the mouth
and judge its pain by its teeth.

With mules, on foot
by airliners and lorries
in our hearts
we carry everything,
harvests, coffins, water,
oil, hydrogen, roads,
flowering lilac and
the earth thrown into the mass grave.

We with our bad foreign news
and another word for milk
what in our single beds
do we know of poetry?

We know as well as the midwives
how women carry children
and give birth,
we know as well as the scholars
what makes a language quiver.

Our freight.
The bringing together of what has been parted
makes a language quiver.
Across millennia and the village street
through tundra and forests
by farewells and bridges
towards the city of our child
everything must be carried.

We contain poetry
as the cattle trucks of the world
carry cattle.
Soon in the sidings
they will sluice them down.

The opposite of to love is not to hate but to separate. If
love and hate have something in common it is because, in
both cases, their energy is that of bringing and holding together—the lover with the loved, the one who hates with the
hated. Both passions are tested by separation.

As soon as space and therefore separateness is the condition of existence, love contests this separation. Love aims to close all distance. Death achieves the same end. Yet whereas love celebrates the unique, the unrepeatable: death destroys them.

Supposing that the universe is an expanding universe, its maximum diameter, the limit of its possible extension, has been calculated as being 25,000 million light years. One light year is 5.8784×10^{12} miles.

Such an extension is beyond our imagination because of the terms in which it is expressed. There is a double separation: that of the statement and that of the numerical isolation.

Elsewhere—in our hearts—we learn the proposition that the force by which space was created may have been an alternating force of expulsion and attraction, extension and passion. This is why, in every language, love is found quoting the stars. But it is also why every cosmology returns to sexuality.

The "cosmic egg" of modern physics and the proposed single original substance of *ylem*—of which one cubic centimeter would weigh, 1,000,000,000,000 kg, and from which all other matter was born—are variants of a theme to be found in most creation myths. Only the nouns change.

Once earth and sky were passionately one, yet nothing had form; everything was virtual. For the world and its forms and its extension to come into existence, earth and sky had to be torn apart and separated.

Love aims to close all distance. Yet if separation and space were annihilated neither loved one nor lover would exist. Between space and love there is the first opposition— that opposition which is contained as energy within the original act of creation.

All theories about origin are either naive or despairing,

from Genesis to Darwin. Yet perhaps one misunderstands their purpose. All origins are unattainable—just as, on a personal scale, it is impossible to imagine a self before conception. Theories of origin are attempts to explain our ongoing relation to the so-evident energy of the universe around us. The energy of our consciousness in all its concentration is continually trying to define itself by and against the energy of the universe in all its incomprehensible extension. Every form of interrogation of the stars has been about this, and every theory of origin is a story invented to describe the experience of being here.

In the beginning was the creator. What followed—if there was to be any story at all—was deployment, extension, space, separateness. Ma femme.

He lies with his head between her legs. How many millions of men have lain like this? How many women, placing a hand on their heads, and smiling reflectively, have thought of birth? Everything here is re-enactment, everything here is return. Home is the return to where distance did not yet count.

DREAM

In a pocket of earth
I buried all the accents
of my mother tongue

there they lie
like needles of pine
assembled by ants

one day the stumbling cry
of another wanderer
may set them alight

then warm and comforted
he will hear all night
the truth as lullaby

Before the railways were built, what took the place of
stations in people's dreams? Perhaps cliffs or wells or a black-
smith's forge? Like a tram or a bus this question is a way of
approaching the railway station.

Of all nineteenth-century buildings, the mainline railway
station was the one in which the ancient sense of destiny was
most fully re-inserted. Stock exchanges, banks, hotels, theaters,
courts were built as pretenses, or, to put it another way, they
were already dreams. The railway station—whatever the
extravagances of its "decorative" architecture—remained stark.
And it remained so because it was a site of arrival and departure, where there was nothing to muffle the significance
of those two events. Coming and going. Meeting and parting.
Dreams welcomed the railway station so readily since it was
already—in other forms—a familiar. The Greek word for
"porter" is *metaphor*. And this is a reminder of how deeply
the act of transporting, of despatch and delivery, is intrinsic to
the imagination.

Seaports are more moderate than mainline railway stations
for, although the distances involved are usually longer, the sea
has not been laid down, like the railtracks, for the sole and

unique purpose of transporting. Airports are too polite; reality is always at one remove in an airport.

In a railway station the impersonal and the intimate co-exist. Destinies are played out. The trains run regularly, according to printed timetables. The lines are inexorable. But for each passenger or for each person who comes to meet or see off a traveler, the train in question has its own portent. The portents can be read close-up, in faces, in details of luggage, in the welcomes and partings as people embrace on the platform.

On that late spring afternoon, few people had come. I was the only one to climb the railings and there, clinging on with one arm, to wait for the train to draw in. In the coaches which passed me, I saw people crowding round the doors, impatient to jump down.

Among the first were some Spaniards, relatives of migrant workers already installed in the city. Their small children, deposited on the platform, looked less bemused than their parents, as if for the children one city was much the same as another, equally familiar and equally unknowable. From a rear coach a man with two Alsatian dogs clambered down. The locomotive, now uncoupled, was driven off, leaving the train stranded.

At that moment I saw you at the end of the platform. You were wearing trousers. On the long platform beside the stranded train, in the vast white diffused late-afternoon light of the rift valley, you looked very small. With your appearance everything changed. Everything from the passage under the railway tracks to the sun setting, from the Arabic numerals on the board which announced the times of the trains, to the gulls perched on a roof, from the invisible stars to the taste of coffee on my palate. The world of circumstance and contingency, into which, long before, I had been born, became like a room. I was home.

You joined the queue of passengers who had to show their

papers to the frontier police. The immigration officer looked you up and down and studied the old photograph in your passport, searching for some trace of resemblance. Finally he nodded, and you held out your arms to me.

To the man selling newspapers by the bus stop I was the same grey-haired foreigner who had bought a paper from him half an hour before. He could see no difference, except that then I had been alone, and now I was accompanied by a woman with a kerchief round her head, who also spoke with a foreign accent.

The apple trees are barking
the beestings on my scalp
mark the rage of the swarm
hold, my honey, your sweetness.

The sky is pressing its thumbs
into my eyes
his constellations are fleeing
hold, my honey, your sweetness.

The endless rain
desiring the mountains as sand
is preparing me for bed
hold, my honey, your sweetness.

During the eighteenth and nineteenth centuries most direct protests against social injustice were in prose. They were reasoned arguments written in the belief that, given time, people would come to see reason, and that, finally, history was on the side of reason. Today this is by no means clear. The outcome is by no means guaranteed. The suffering of the present and the past is unlikely to be redeemed by a future era of universal happiness. And evil is a constant ineradicable reality. All this means that the resolution—the coming to terms with the sense to be given to life—cannot be deferred. The future cannot be trusted. The moment of truth is now. And more and more it will be poetry, rather than prose, that receives this truth. Prose is far more *trusting* than poetry; poetry speaks to the immediate wound.

The boon of language is not tenderness. All that it holds, it holds with exactitude and without pity, even a term of endearment; the word is impartial: the usage is all. The boon of language is that *potentially* it is complete, it has the potentiality of holding with words the totality of human experience —everything that has occurred and everything that may occur. It even allows space for the unspeakable. In this sense one can say of language that it is potentially the only human home, the only dwelling place that cannot be hostile to man. For prose this home is a vast territory, a country which it crosses through a network of tracks, paths, highways; for poetry this home is concentrated on a single center, a single voice, and this voice is simultaneously that of an announcement and a response to it.

One can say anything to language. This is why it is a listener, closer to us than any silence or any god. Yet its very openness can signify indifference. (The indifference of language is continually solicited and employed in bulletins, legal records, communiqués, files.) Poetry addresses language in such a way as to close this indifference and to incite a caring.

How does poetry incite this caring? What is the labor of poetry?

By this I do not mean the work involved in writing a poem, but the work of the written poem itself. Every authentic poem contributes to the labor of poetry. And the task of this unceasing labor is to bring together what life has separated or violence has torn apart. Physical pain can usually be lessened or stopped only by action. All other human pain, however, is caused by one form or another of separation. And here the act of assuagement is less direct. Poetry can repair no loss but it defies the space which separates. And it does this by its continual labor of reassembling what has been scattered. Three thousand five hundred years ago, an Egyptian poet was writing:

O my beloved
how sweet it is
to go down
and bathe in the pool
before your eyes
letting you see how
my drenched linen dress
marries
the beauty of my body
Come, look at me.

Poetry's impulse to use metaphor, to discover resemblance, is not to make comparisons (all comparisons as such are hierarchical) or to diminish the particularity of any event; it is to discover those correspondences of which the sum total would be proof of the indivisible totality of existence. To this totality poetry appeals, and its appeal is the opposite of a sentimental one; sentimentality always pleads for an exemption, for something which *is* divisible.

Apart from reassembling by metaphor, poetry reunites by its *reach*. It equates the reach of a feeling with the reach of the universe; after a certain point the type of extremity involved becomes unimportant and all that matters is its degree; by their degree alone extremities are joined. Anna Akhmatova:

> I bear equally with you
> the black permanent separation.
> Why are you crying? Rather give me your hand,
> promise to come again in a dream.
> You and I are a mountain of grief.
> You and I will never meet on this earth.
> If only you could send me at midnight
> a greeting through the stars.

To argue here that the subjective and objective are confused is to return to an empirical view which the extent of present suffering challenges; strangely enough it is to claim an unjustified privilege.

Poetry makes language care because it renders everything intimate. This intimacy is the result of the poem's labor, the result of the bringing-together-into-intimacy of every act and noun and event and perspective to which the poem refers. There is often nothing more substantial to place against the cruelty and indifference of the world than this caring.

From where does Pain come to us?
From where does he come?
He has been the brother of our visions
from time immemorial
And the guide of our rhymes.

writes the poet Nazik al Mal'-ika.

To break the silence of events, to speak of experience however bitter or lacerating, to put into words, is to discover the hope that these words may be heard, and that when heard, the events will be judged. This hope is of course at the origin of prayer, and prayer—as well as labor—was probably at the origin of speech itself. Of all uses of language, it is poetry that preserves most purely the memory of this origin.

Every poem that works as a poem is original. And *original* has two meanings: it means a return to the origin, the first which engendered everything that followed; and it means that which has never occurred before. In poetry, and in poetry alone, the two senses are united in such a way that they are no longer contradictory.

Nevertheless poems are not simple prayers. Even a religious poem is not exclusively and uniquely addressed to God. Poetry is addressed to language itself. In a lamentation, words lament loss to their language. Poetry is addressed to language in a comparable but wider way.

To put into words is to find the hope that the words will be heard and the events they describe judged. Judged by God or judged by history. Either way the judgment is distant. Yet the language, which is immediate and which is sometimes wrongly thought of as being only a means, the language offers, obstinately and mysteriously, its own judgment when it is addressed as poetry. This judgment is distinct from that of any moral code, yet it promises, within its acknowledgment of what it has heard, a distinction between good and evil—as though language itself had been created to preserve just that distinction!

We woke up in a friend's house where there was a piano. We had slept on a mattress on the floor. The piano was in the room below. The two children of the house were playing an exercise before going to school. An exercise for four hands. Sometimes they stumbled and began the phrase again.

If ours were the eighteenth century, when questions opened idly like doors onto gardens, I might ask you: Do you remember? But in our century, when only evil and indifference are limitless, we cannot afford unnecessary questions; rather, we need to defend ourselves with whatever there is to hand of certainty. I know that you remember.

The two children were playing lightly and dutifully and the notes filled the house. You were lying with your back to me, your breasts in my hands. Neither of us stirred. The music commanded a little listening and we listened—just as one can gaze at the wallpaper in a hotel room without really looking at it. Waking up to that music played lightly and dutifully by the children before going to school was the nearest we shall ever be, my heart, to waking up at home before we left.

In that town,
across the water
where all has been seen
and the bricks are cherished like sparrows,
in that town like a letter from home
read again and again in a port,
in that town with its library of tiles
and its addresses recalled by Johannes Vermeer
who died in debt,
in that town across the water
where the dead take the census
and there are no vacant rooms
for his gaze occupies them all,
where the sky is waiting
to have news of a birth,
in that town which pours from the eyes
of those who left it,
there
between two chimes of the morning,
when fish are sold in the square
and the maps on the walls
show the depth of the sea,
in that town
I am preparing for your arrival.

What reconciles me to my own death more than anything else is the image of a place: a place where your bones and mine are buried, thrown, uncovered, together. They are strewn there pell-mell. One of your ribs leans against my skull. A metacarpal of my left hand lies inside your pelvis. (Against my broken ribs your breast like a flower.) The hundred bones of our feet are scattered like gravel. It is strange that this image of our proximity, concerning as it does mere phosphate of calcium, should bestow a sense of peace. Yet it does. With you I can imagine a place where to be phosphate of calcium is enough.

Page 21: The poem by Yevgeny Vinokurov is from Daniel Weissbort, ed., *Post-War Russian Poetry* (New York: Penguin Books, 1974), p. 103. Translation by Daniel Weissbort.

Page 82: The quotation is from Danilo Dolci, *Sicilian Lives*, trans. Justin Vitiello (New York: Pantheon Books, 1981), p. 209.

Page 85: The poem by Cafavy is from *Poems by C. P. Cafavy*, trans. John Mavrogordato (London: Hogarth Press, 1971), p. 79.

Page 97: The poem by Anna Akhmatova is from Daniel Weissbort, ed., *Post-War Russian Poetry* (New York: Penguin Books, 1974). Translation by Richard McKane.

Page 98: The poem by Nazik al Mal'-ika is from Issa J. Boullata, ed. and trans., *Modern Arab Poets: 1950–1975* (Washington, D.C.: Three Continents, 1976).

ABOUT THE AUTHOR

John Berger, born in London in 1926, is well known as a novelist, essayist, art critic, film scriptwriter. His many books, innovative in form and far-reaching in their historical and political insight, include *About Looking, Ways of Seeing, Art and Revolution, The Success and Failure of Picasso, Another Way of Telling, Pig Earth,* and the award-winning novel *G.*

He now lives and works in a small French peasant community. This milieu is the setting of *Into Their Labours,* a three-part project which evokes, in fiction form, the peasant's odyssey from village to metropolis.